THE RICH GET RICHER AND THE POOR WRITE PROPOSALS

by Nancy Mitiguy
of the Citizen Involvement Training Project (CITP)

The Citizen Involvement Training Project (CITP) is a collaborative project of the Division of Continuing Education and the Cooperative Extension Service at the University of Massachusetts at Amherst. CITP is funded by a major grant from the W.K. Kellogg Foundation of Battle Creek, Michigan, with additional support from the Blanchard and Polaroid Foundations.

Cover by Robbie Gordon

ISBN 0-934210-02-0
1st printing, September, 1978
2nd printing, July 1979
3rd printing, March, 1980

Contributing Artists:

Brenda Yellock
Bonnie Acker

(plus artwork from
Community Press
Features and
Albums by
Caran d'Ache)

Stats:

Bob Biagi

Typesetting:

Campus Center
Print Shop,
University of
Massachusetts

Design/Layout:

Nancy Mitiguy
Britt Warren
Robbie Gordon

Editing:

Robbie Gordon
Ken Walker

CITP Staff:

Eduardo Aponte
Bob Biagi
Duane Dale
Al Goldin
John Gondek
Robbie Gordon
Sally Habana-Hafner
Dean Hudson
Diana Krauth
Dave Magnani
Robin Miller
Stan Rosenberg
Greg Speeter
Jay Walsh

Acknowledgements

Special thanks to Robbie Gordon and Rick Feldman for their
encouragement, Dave Magnani for his questions, and
Sally Habana Hafner for taking care of the many details and
keeping us on our toes.

Our thanks to the reviewers of this manual:

Rick Feldman: Cooperative Extension Service, Amherst, Mass.
Ginny Gordon: VISTA Resource Mobilizer, Springfield, Mass.
Mary Kasper: Hampshire Community Action, Northampton, Mass.
Diana Krauth: Grantsmanship Center, Washington, D.C.
Susan Markman: Rape Information and Prevention Project, Northampton,
                Mass.
Sister Rhonda Meister S.P.: Campaign for Human Development, Springfield,
                Mass.
Bill Seretta: Center for Human Ecology Studies, Freeport, Maine
Gracelaw Simmons: Associated Foundation of Greater Boston, Boston, Mass.
Judy Sutphen: Haymarket Foundation, Cambridge, Mass.

Their recommendations were all excellent and incorporated into the manual
where possible; any shortcomings are, of course, the responsibility of the
author.

Table of Contents

"FOLD THUMB (A) OVER FINGERS (B,C,D,E) MAKING TIGHT FIST. THRUST ASSEMBLY FORWARD..."

CPF

The Citizen Involvement Training Project

The Citizen Involvement Training Project (CITP) provides training workshops, materials, and consultations to citizen groups throughout Massachusetts. The staff of nine includes specialists in organizing, fund-raising, group process, planning methods, information gathering, social change and adult education, and offers bilingual training as well.

CITP services include workshops and consultation, a 1000 volume Citizen Involvement Library (available to individuals and citizen groups), staff-generated manuals (such as this) and a *Training of Trainers* workshop series intended to help citizen groups establish their own training components in their communities.

Citizen Involvement Training Project
138 Hasbrouck
Division of Continuing Education
University of Massachusetts
Amherst, Massachusetts 01003
(413) 545-3450

About Citizen "Training"

The word "training" may bring to mind a lion trainer, or a sargeant drilling an army — the sort of learning where one person is in charge and the trainee is in a passive or submissive role. "On-the-job training" brings forth a different image — that of a worker learning new skills relevant to the job (s)he is doing or about to begin. Citizen involve-ment training is, more precisely, on-the-job training.

Citizen involvement training consists of people learning how to identify and then acquire the skills they need as citizen group members. Ideally, it is "active learning," since people do not tend to learn to be more powerful by taking a passive role in the learning process. So the "curricula" for citizens who want to have a say in decision-making consists of role-plays and simulations, diagnostic interviews and checklists, small group discussions centered around specific issues, or perhaps a support group of sorts, to give the encouragement a group needs to go out and do something — consciously.

About the CITP Manual Series

Usually, when CITP conducts a workshop for a citizen group, the CITP staff members first sit down with the group to discuss the problem and needs. These initial sessions consist of probing questions which are aimed at helping the group identify root causes as well as immediate, readily ap-

parent problems. Many groups come in feeling that they need help with fund-raising, only to find that the need for funds is a symptom of a deeper problem — perhaps poor planning or a weak decision-making structure.

After discussing the problems and needs, the CITP staff and representatives of the group or agency then sit down to design a workshop or workshop series to suit those needs.

This manual, as well as others in the series, is intended to help citizen groups set up their own on-the-job training activities tailored to their individual needs, issues, learning styles and experiences. In writing these manuals we have used what we have learned through our experience with hundreds of citizen groups.

It is hoped that these manuals will be used to help orient new members to an organization, and will be an integral part of membership/staff development. Some organizations are reluctant to spend time on training activities, at least at first, before the merits have been proven. The reluctance is appropriate; training can be a diversion from the real concerns of the group. But training activities can emphasize the development of analytical capabilities and appropriate strategies.

If you are the one introducing training exercises to your group, you might first spend some time discussing these reluctancies or individual learning preferences. Then again, you may want to let the proof of the pudding rest in the tasting.

About the Exercises

There are several exercises and sections in this manual which you might want to duplicate, adapt to suit your group's needs, or use as a smaller, condensed version of a "training workbook" for the entire group.

It's assumed that the trainer who uses these materials has had some fund-raising experience, or at least will have read this manual and some of the resource materials prior to trying the exercises. Trainers should be prepared to do the following:

- Determine the training needs and interests of participants.

- Recruit participants to attend training or staff development sessions.

- Introduce and explain the exercises.

- Lead discussions, keeping them focused and summarizing participants' ideas.

- Help the group determine "next steps," whether it's specific tasks to be done, continuation of the discussion, or a re-assessment of training needs.

You might want to refer to the CITP manual entitled **Training of Trainers** for a more in-depth look at the role of a trainer.

Trainers should also determine the number of participants and the amount of time required for each exercise. The amount of time to be spent should be determined before starting the exercise and should take into consideration the available time and interest level of participants. We suggest that the exercises be done in small groups (a maximum of ten people) to ensure the active participation of all members. Materials required for the activities are minimal. Newsprint or large sheets of paper should be taped to walls so that participants' ideas can be recorded during the activity. Other necessay materials include magic markers, paper and pens. For a few exercises, index cards are needed.

Whatever way you use the manual, we hope you will tailor it to suit your own needs and learning styles. All exercises in the manual appear on single pages so that you can duplicate them easily; exercises are denoted as such so that you will know they are optional as you read through each chapter.

Definition of Terms

Fund-raising — the word "fund-raising" is used throughout the manual instead of "grantsmanship" because a good portion of citizen group funds come from membership dues and events — activities that do not involve grants.

Fundraiser — the word "fundraiser" is intended to mean any person(s), paid or unpaid, who is raising money for citizen groups. It's assumed that fund-raising is probably not a full-time position and that fundraisers have multiple responsibilities, such as co-ordinating programs, community organizing, providing services or managing financial affairs.

Fund-raising skills — this is a phrase that is frequently used but rarely defined. The definition of "fund-raising skills" used in this book is based on the author's concept of what it takes to raise money for citizen groups. Those skills include:

- long and short term planning

- conceptualizing programs — taking an idea and designing a program

- writing and speaking

- listening

- dreaming — generating program options

- delegating tasks to others and asking for help when it's needed

- research

- negotiating with funding sources

- time management — establishing work priorities

- creativity

- assertiveness

Emphasis is intentionally placed on planning, since fund-raising consists of finding support for *future* programs.

Introduction

Like soldiers going into battle, fundraisers race about armed with proposals, concept papers, documentation, budgets, newspaper clippings, endless lists of deadlines and appointment calendars that have no more white spaces left. They tend to frequent new skyscrapers, law offices, banks and large government office buildings. Occasionally, you'll see one standing on a street corner grinning, having just received a "We are pleased to inform you" letter. More often, you'll see them glumly flipping through a stack of rejection letters or silently rehearsing for their next appointment. Behind the scenes, there's all the research (those long hours pouring through the sterling prose of the **Federal Register**), the multiple drafts of proposals, the planning necessary for this year's activities, the bake sales, the cash flow problem, the budget deficits and all the rest.

The purpose of this unit is to help you develop your own strategies and skills with some analysis about how fund-raising for citizen groups fits into the scheme of things. Every fundraiser has faced at least one of the situations above, so the main focus here is to explore some solutions to problems that are common to most fundraisers and to suggest some preventive measures for avoiding the usual pitfalls. *The objectives of this manual are:*

- *To demystify the fund-raising process.*

- *To provide basic information about fund-raising and opportunities for readers to "learn by doing."*

- *To increase the reader's confidence and capacity for raising money for citizen groups.*

- *To enable the reader to begin designing and implementing his or her own fund-raising strategy.*

Now, how about you? What do you want to learn from this unit?
Take a few minutes and list the **specific** things you hope to learn.

1.

2.

3.

4.

5.

If you had trouble with that one or you weren't very specific, think
about the things you do well and the things you think you need work
on. You might want to refer to the **Table of Contents** or skim through
through the **Steps in the Fund-Raising Process.**

Fund-raising skills I have	Skills I don't have or need to improve
1.	1.
2.	2.
3.	3.
4.	4.
5.	5.

Keep this list close by as you go through this manual, concentrating
on those areas in the right hand column.

Wealth
and Fund-Raising

This is an affluent country — the gross national product has doubled
in 10 years and, as of this writing, is close to the $2 trillion mark.
And yet, the number of people without jobs has doubled in 11 years
to six million. The February 1978 average weekly take-home pay
was $92.70 (expressed in terms of what it was worth in 1967 — an
increase of $1.84 in 11 years). In 1962, the wealth (cash, cars, pro-
perty, investments) of almost half of American households was $5,000
or less. In the same year, 2.65% of the households owned 65% of
investment assets. This is a wealthy country — with a wealthy
minority.

Such imbalances are reflected in both the need for fundraisers and the tensions they face. Many citizen groups who are trying to change the plight of the poor and powerless find themselves turning to funding sources that are controlled by the wealthy. This is often seen as a form of redistributing the wealth. Citizen groups need to ask whether or not the relation to wealth of the powerless really does change as a result of this kind of funding. In a sense, fund-raising perpetuates the status quo. Centers of economic power remain intact and the poor remain poor. Other people see raising money from the wealthy as co-optation — although some short term needs are satisfied through such donations, the group is unable to move toward more substantive changes. Still others see this type of funding as purely benevolent — a pluralistic approach ("everyone working together") to solve society's problems.

There aren't any comfortable solutions to this situation. Fund-raising is a short-term strategy for changing the plight of the poor and powerless. It's a means to an end — no more than that.

Discussion Questions:

- *What is the problem your group is trying to address (e.g. unemployment, rural housing, health care)?*

- *What are the causes of the problem? For example, are people unemployed because they don't have skills or because there aren't enough jobs to go around? Why do they not have the required skills? Why aren't there enough jobs to go around?*

- *Based on your analysis of the problem, from what sources should your group concentrate its fund-raising efforts?*

    - Government: tax dollars

    - Churches: church membership

    - Grassroots Organizations: community residents/group's membership

    - Foundations: investment assets/unearned income

    - Corporations: profits

- *In what ways will your fund-raising result in shifts of power and economic control, if at all?*

- *How will your fund-raising effort affect the nature of the group's activities? Will funding change the focus of your organization from advocacy activities to providing services?*

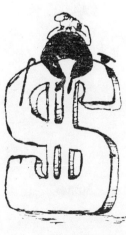

Berke Breathed
The Progressive

6

- *Who will benefit from the fund-raising effort?*

  - poor people

  - middle class

  - upper middle class

  - wealthy

  - your own agency

- *How will people benefit from your fund-raising efforts?*

  - jobs

  - services

  - economic gains

  - economic and/or political power

  - other:

  - other:

Umbasi/ Black Scholar/cpf

CLIMBING THE AMERICAN SUPER "STRUCTURE"

Steps in the Fund-Raising Process

by Art Finley

Fundraisers are probably the most insecure lot on this planet, unless of course you meet one of the presumptuous ones. Most fundraisers have an insatiable urge to find the key that fits the magic funding door. No one's found it yet so it's safe to assume that there isn't one. That leaves fundraisers with the task of increasing their own knowledge and skills. Here are a few things you can do to begin:

1. **Do it!** They say that experience is the best teacher and it's true with raising money.

2. **Talk with other fundraisers.** Everyone has had different experiences and has his or her own idea about what works and what doesn't. Compare the ideas of others with your own — it gets the creative juices flowing.

3. **Keep a journal.** Record both goofs and successes as you gain experience. This is particularly helpful for other people who are also fund-raising for the organization; and it may give you a chuckle someday when you look back and see all the silly things you did.

4. **Read about it.** This may be one of the dullest things you could do because most of the written material on fund-raising is boring. Two publications on fund-raising stand out, though, because they dare to be interesting and witty — the **Grantsmanship Center News** and **The Grass Roots Fundraising Book,** by Joan Flanagan. Try these for starters and then consult other materials listed in the **Resource** section of this manual.

5. **Visit information centers.** Public libraries, The Foundation Center and its regional collections, and government agencies are all good sources of information on funding. See also the list of resource centers under *Researching Possible Funding Sources* in this manual.

On the following page you'll find a diagram of the steps in the fund-raising process for both grant writing and grassroots fund-raising. An explanation of the grants process follows the diagram; see the *Grassroots Fund-Raising* section for information on that process. In some cases, the sequence of the steps will need to be changed to suit your own situation and you may need to add a few steps, but these are the basic ones. The model is used here to spark some thinking and discussion about what it takes to raise money for citizen groups.

8

Steps in the Fund-Raising Process:

THE GRANTS PROCESS

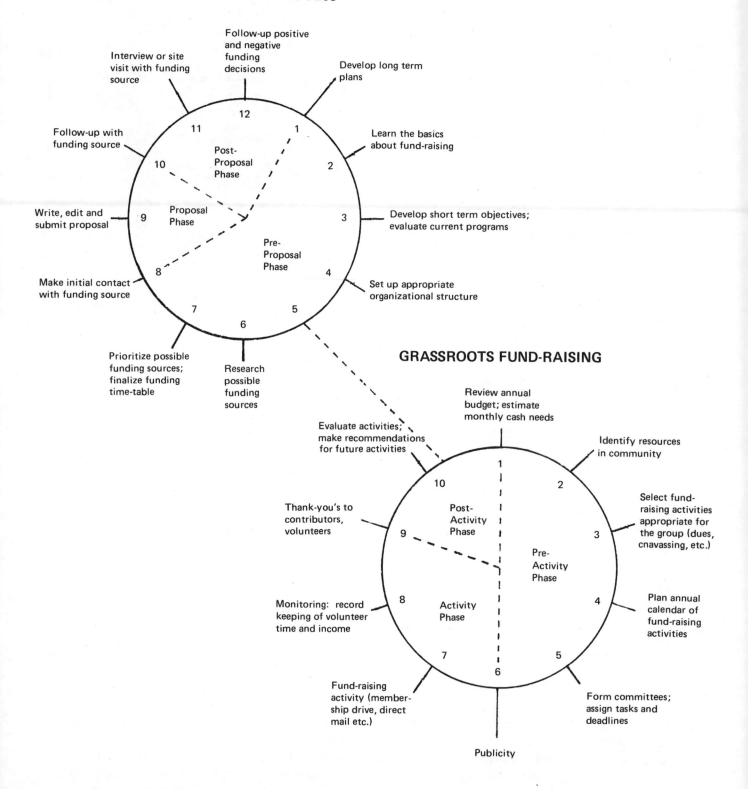

GRASSROOTS FUND-RAISING

*Adapted from a model prepared by the Institute for Fundraising in California.

Steps 1 & 3: Long- and Short-Term Planning

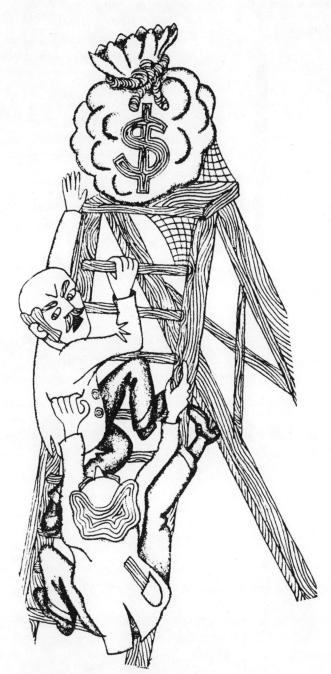

With the organization's chorus chanting, "Yup, yup, we need money — go get 'em champ," many fund-raisers run off scheming and dreaming of the splashiest benefit, a well-conceived proposal and lots of money in the bank. Sooner or later, the fund-raiser returns asking, "But what do we want money for?"

All too often, especially with new and struggling organizations, swelling the checking account is seen as an end, rather than a means to an end. Money is raised without considering how appropriate it is for the organization and the effect it will have on the organization.

Here are some common statements made by fund-raisers that indicate a lack of organizational planning:

- *"I'll find out what kind of projects are being funded, then we'll decide what projects we'll do."*

- *"I've had very little direction from the organization about its plan for for the next year(s)."*

- *"I feel like I'm working in a vacuum — inventing programs and work plans while I write proposals."*

Exercise:
Introductory Planning Activity

Logically, it makes sense for organizations to be clear about what they hope to accomplish before an effort is made to raise money. But it's not always that easy. There's often resistance to attempts to predict what the future will be. There may be resistance to planning itself — it's sometimes perceived as a bureaucratic exercise. Or there may be philosophical differences among individuals in a group. Or a lack of knowledge about how to plan.

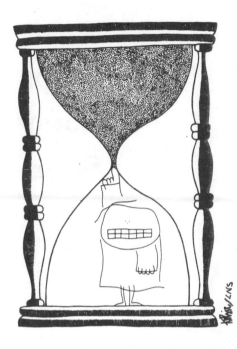

Finally, planning takes time, and most citizen groups have enough to do dealing with the present, let alone the future.

While each of these is a barrier to effective program planning, they're not insurmountable. Getting the members or staff to commit themselves to planning is the first critical step. The focus of this activity is on encouraging members to discuss their personal motivation for joining the group.

The Process:

1. Select a discussion leader.

2. Write the six questions below on separate sheets of newsprint and tape them to the the wall. The questions will help people dream a little and express their own personal hopes.

  - *Why did you join this organization?*

  - *What would you like to see the organization accomplish over the next several years?*

  - *What **shouldn't** the organization be doing over the next few years?*

  - *If money were no object, list all the things you'd like to see happen in the next year.*

  - *What are the goals of the organization?*

  - *What specific activities are you most interested in doing?*

3. Ask each member of the group to circulate around the room, writing down responses to each question *on the newsprint*. Allow 15-30 minutes, or until the exercise begins to break down and people are milling aimlessly about.

4. Divide up into small groups of four or five people each. Ask each group to compile a list of long-term goals, using ideas from the newsprint. Make sure that everyone agrees on a definition for the phrase "long-term." For example, you might define long-term as 10 years, 50 years or a century. Allow approximately 15 minutes for each group to compile a list of goals, recording them on newsprint.

5. Hang each group's newsprint on the wall so everyone can see them. Summarize each goal so that everyone understands what they mean. Combine goals that are similar, rewording them when necessary.

6. Ask each person to select the three goals that seem to be the most appropriate ones for the organization. Beginning at the top of the goals list, ask how many people have selected each goal, reminding participants that they have only three votes.

7. This process may need to be repeated several times, whittling down the list of goals each time to exclude those that received no votes.

8. Discuss the results, checking for completeness and to see whether or not participants agree with the results.

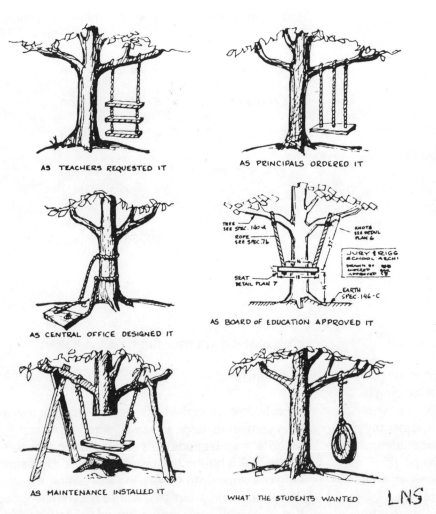

AS TEACHERS REQUESTED IT

AS PRINCIPALS ORDERED IT

AS CENTRAL OFFICE DESIGNED IT

AS BOARD OF EDUCATION APPROVED IT

AS MAINTENANCE INSTALLED IT

WHAT THE STUDENTS WANTED

LNS

Suggested follow-up:

This activity represents the beginning step in planning. There's obviously more to effective planning so consult the Resource section for a more in-depth look at ways to develop programs, particularly if members of the organization have had a difficult time stating what the future of the group should be.

Reprinted from Workforce

Step 2:
Learning the Basics about Fund-Raising

Frequently, citizen groups adopt a funding strategy based on misconceptions about different funding sources. A statement like, "Let's get some foundation money because there's lots of it and it's easier than having bake sales," usually indicates a lack of basic information on who's got how much money. Here are some basic facts on funding:

Funding Source	Annual Contributions (1977)	
Government	$ 45.60	billion (categorical grants only — 1976)
Individuals	$ 29.50	billion
Churches	$ 9.34	billion
Bequests	$ 2.12	billion
Foundations	$ 2.01	billion
Corporations	$ 1.57	billion
United Way	$927.00	million

Government:

Obviously, the largest funding source is the public sector. Competition for government funding is intense and citizen groups invariably find themselves competing with similar groups across the country. In some cases, they're also competing with local governments and large non profit institutions (like hospitals and universities) that have sizable staffs devoted to fund-raising. Raising money from the public sector is also time-consuming, a factor that is troublesome for citizen groups who don't have full-time fundraisers.

Individuals:

Next in line are individuals, people like you and me who contribute large and small amounts to our favorite organizations. It's worth noting that half of the $29.5 billion total is given to churches and religious organizations, leaving $14 billion for United Way, education, hospitals, and social welfare groups. But that's still more money than foundations and corporate grants combined . . .

Churches:

The $9.3 billion spent by churches and religious-related institutions includes a substantial amount for church-sponsored schools and hospitals. The precise amount donated by churches to nonreligious institutions is not known but is considerably less than the $9.3 billion figure. However, this is a potential funding source that many citizen groups have not yet explored.

Bequests:

These are gifts designated by wealthy individuals to specific institutions, payable when the donor dies. The bulk of bequests is given to universities, hospitals, symphonies, museums and large, well-established institutions in general. Most citizen groups don't have the personal contact or legal expertise needed to solicit these gifts.

Foundations:

Then come some 26,000 foundations who each year are required to "pay out" 5% of their assets to tax-exempt organizations. Because all foundation money is invested, the amount distributed varies slightly from year to year, depending on the general health of the stock market. The $2.01 billion in grants is a figure that surprises many novice fundraisers who've heard about the Ford Foundation (total grants of $173 million) and assume that all other foundations are large and distribute lots of money. However, of the 26,000 foundations, 20,000 are family foundations that control only 15% of total foundation assets.

Corporations:

Total grants made by the 1.7 million U.S. corporations hovers at a low $1.57 billion. This does not include in-kind contributions made to nonprofit groups — products, office furniture, printing, donated time of employees and use of corporate facilities — which add roughly $1 billion more.

Although corporations are permitted to deduct up to 5% of their taxable income on "charitable contributions," total contributions average only 1% of pre-tax profits. Some people think that there is "room for growth" because legally corporations can give more money than they do. Others argue that there's no real incentive for corporations to give more, and that they probably will continue at the 1% level in the future.

United Way:

With $927,000,000 in allocations to social welfare, health, and recreation/youth agencies, United Way generally sticks with well-established, "safe" organizations, such as the Red Cross, hospitals, Boy Scouts, YM- and YWCAs and the like. As with corporations and most foundations, social change groups have been excluded from the list of grantees.

Once an organization receives United Way funding, it usually continues to receive support year after year, decreasing the chances for other organizations to become accepted as United Way grantees. One happy note is that some United Ways are starting to pick up the tab for day care centers, which have been having an increasingly difficult time getting funding from other sources.

This was the briefest of brief summaries, so here are some things you can do to increase your repertoire of basic facts:

- Turn to sections of this manual for more information about specific types of funding sources.

- Read through the short **Giving USA,** the annual report prepared by the American Association of Fund-Raising Counsel, Inc. (500 Fifth Avenue, New York, NY 10036). It gives the latest statistics and trends on individual, foundation and corporate gifts.

- Pick sections of the **Research Papers,** sponsored by the Commission on Private Philanthropy and Public Needs (published by U.S. Department of Treasury; available form the Government Printing Office or government bookstores). The volume, **Philanthropic Fields of Interest** (Volume II, Parts I and II), is the most relevant for citizen groups. Although bulky, it has several enlightening papers on foundation and corporate funding of minority, women and social change groups.

- Read every issue of the **Grantsmanship Center News** (1015 West Olympic Boulevard, Los Angeles, CA 90015).

With some of these facts under your belt, you're in a better position to plan a funding strategy.

14

Exercise:
Where Will Your Funding Come From?

The purpose of this activity is to help summarize your knowledge of various funding options and begin developing a funding strategy for your organization. This activity may be done by an individual, but it is better suited to a group of people who have had some fundraising experience. Therefore, if you're the only one in your organization who has the foggiest notion of what raising money is all about, carry this chart with you when you talk with fundraisers from other citizen groups, asking them for their comments.

Suggested Follow-up:

Further discussion will help members of your organization understand some general characteristics of different types of funding sources. It's likely, however, that some research will be necessary before the group can make a final decision about appropriate types of funding sources. See Step No. 6 for information on research techniques.

The Process:

1. On a blackboard or large sheet of paper, reconstruct the chart below:

Sources of Funding

	Government	Corporations	Foundations	Churches	United Way	Grassroots (members, events)
Advantages						
Disadvantages						

2. Take 15-30 minutes to solicit everyone's comments about the various disadvantages and advantages of raising funds from these sources. Comments like, "advantage: source gives large grants," "disadvantage: strings attached to grants," are what you're looking for — general statements about what it's like to raise funds from each type of funding source.

3. Use the results to begin the discussion of where your organization will concentrate its fund-raising efforts.

Step 4:
Setting up
an Appropriate
Organizational
Structure

Citizen groups come in all sizes, shapes and structures. But not all shapes and structures are acceptable to every funding source. In this section there are several activities focusing on *organizational structure, as it relates to fund-raising.*

Some funding sources, like most corporations and foundations, will only make grants to tax-exempt organizations. Composition of boards of directors is also likely to play a role in the "fundability" of an organization. Finally, whether a group concentrates on "advocacy" or providing services can also be a factor in funding decisions. There aren't any hard-and-fast rules, so it's advisable to consult similar organizations about their experience. Also consult an attorney.

Exercise:
Should your Organization Incorporate or Not?

Incorporation is the process of forming a legal entity — for most citizen groups, this is a nonprofit corporation. Organizations that incorporate do so in the state(s) in which they operate. In Massachusetts, the process is handled by the Office of the State Secretary, Corporations Division. Groups who wish to incorporate must file "articles of organization" with the Office, along with a $30 filing fee. The next step involves obtaining a tax status from the Internal Revenue Service. Publication 557 ("How to Apply for Recognition of Exemption for an Organization") and Form 1023 (the application form) are available from regional Internal Revenue Service offices.

With members of the policy-making board of your organization, discuss the following structural options, using the questions as a guide.

The Process:

1. Select a discussion leader.

2. Pass out copies of the options.

3. Divide into small discussion groups of four or five people.

4. Discuss each option, concentrating on the advantages and disadvantages for your organization.

5. Summarize the small group discussions. *Ask for specific recommendations on the appropriate structure for your group, weighing the pros and cons until consensus is reached.*

6. Before a final decision is made, a lawyer familiar with nonprofit regulations should be consulted.

Options

- A group of people get together, pick a name for the newly formed organization (optional), and go to work as volunteers.

- A group forms, works for several years, then incorporates.

- An unincorporated group works under the umbrella of an existing, tax-exempt organization, so funds can "flow through" the tax-exempt group. Often called a "conduit" or "channeling agency."

- A group forms and immediately files its incorporation papers and then its tax-exempt application.

- A group doing workplace or community organizing sets up a separate tax-exempt organization.

Comments

If no funds are required or if proceeds from fund-raising events or dues cover the group's costs, fine. If other funding is sought, especially from corporations, the government, or foundations, not being incorporated and tax-exempt will be a definite liability.

This option is desirable if funds will be sought from sources outside the group's membership. Waiting a few years enables the group to establish a "track record" of accomplishments before seeking outside funding.

Usually seen by funding sources as a temporary situation, this option is frequently used while a group is waiting to receive its tax-exempt status. Occasionally, problems/conflicts have arisen between the group and its sponsor, so care must be taken to maintain a good relationship (a written contract spelling out responsibilities of each party can be helpful). If all funds come from individuals, members and fund-raising events, this structure may be sufficient, since gifts to the tax-exempt organization are deductible. Most churches and some foundations find this structure satisfactory.

This enables the group to approach funding sources outside its membership. Unlike the second option, the group has not yet established a "track record," so will have to work on getting established in the community, while it is busy raising funds.

This is a good structure if the group's activities are "controversial," enabling it to continue to take action or an advocacy role, yet receive funds through its tax-exempt arm (usually for more innocuous activities like research and publications). It also enables individuals to deduct their donations (provided they itemize deductions on their tax returns).

Discussion Questions:

- *Why is the selected option(s) appropriate for the kind of activities the group is undertaking?*

- *If your group is contemplating changing your structure, why do people feel the structure needs to be changed at this point in time?*

- *How will a change in the group's structure help the group achieve its goals more effectively?*

Exercise:
Who Should be on your Policy-Making Board?

SUE

Drawing by Aline Fruhauf, Baseball Team
Reprinted from Graphic Works of the American
Thirties, DaCapo Press

A subject of much debate, the composition of policy-making boards deserves some serious thinking. Since the board members are frequently involved in fund-raising, who is on the board is an important question.

This activity focuses on board composition. The discussion could be one of the agenda items at a regular board meeting or you could include staff and members at a special meeting.

Discussion Questions:

- *How does the composition of the board of directors affect the goals and activities of the group?*

- *What is the rationale for changing the composition of the board?*

- *What positive changes will each option result in for the board? for the organization? for the members?*

The Process:

1. Divide up into groups of five to eight people.

2. Select a discussion leader for each group.

3. Write each option at the top of a large sheet of paper. Then write "Advantages" on the left side and "Disadvantages" on the right side, giving you five sheets of paper in all.

4. Spend 10 minutes making sure everyone understands what each option means and ask if there are any other possibilities.

5. Discuss each option for at least 30 minutes, listing the advantages and disadvantages of each.

6. Select the one option that seems most relevant to your group's situation.

7. Compare the selections made by each small group, with a spokesperson stating why the selection was made (10 min.).

8. If others chose different options, discuss *why* each was selected (the criteria used) and *how* each *will affect* the organization.

Options for Board Composition

Comments

- Maintain the present composition of the board (what is it; are there specific criteria for board membership—age, sex, race, religion, level of interest, skills?).

Review the criteria for board membership. Note problems and differences of opinion about board composition.

- Mixture of skills/perspectives (accounting, legal, fund-raising, business, community people, "professionals in the field").

Some foundations, corporations and government agencies prefer to see people with technical skills on boards, thinking that it increases the stability and capability of the organization to manage programs well and handle money responsibly.

- The Board should be restricted to community people, organization members, or people from the "affected class."

Some funding sources, like the Campaign for Human Development (Catholic Church), require the involvement of poor people, or the "affected class," in the decision-making process.

- The Board should only be composed of staff or members; no one from the "outside."

Some funding sources are likely to be concerned about whether or not technical skills are available to the group if there are no "outside" board members. If staff make up the board, grantors may wonder about accountability.

- Inclusion of a few "name people," especially business people and politicians who lend their names as supporters but do not participate in decision-making.

This is an option that stirs great debate. Some funding sources look at a list of board members to see what names they recognize; others prefer to see people with skills that will help the management of the organization.

Possible Follow-Up:

If your group decides to alter its present board structure, you may want to amend the organization's bylaws. For example, if you want only active people on the board, you could include a stipulation that board members who miss two consecutive regular meetings be asked to resign. If you already have a board and can't change its composition, you might want to set up an advisory board.

Step 5:
Grassroots Fund-Raising:
Developing Community Support

Sketched by J.P. Hoffman, Harper's Weekly, 1869.

Of all the steps in fund-raising, this is one of the most important, following closely on the heels of program planning. Without local support, citizen groups would soon become an endangered species. Why? Well, if you can't convince people in the community that your group is worth supporting, then it's even more difficult to convince funding sources outside the community that the group deserves financial help.

Perhaps a more significant effect of local fund-raising is the kind of accountability that is built into the organization. Support from members and the community is possible only when programs match the needs and interests of the community. When programs seem irrelevant or ineffective, community interest is likely to dwindle, if not disappear altogether.

But good programs do die — why? It's a question worth asking before embarking on a new program. The next few activities focus on problems that many groups face when they attempt to build community support for their programs.

For a more extensive look at the various types of grassroots fund-raising, see the chapter, *Grassroots Fund-Raising* (particularly the sections on membership dues, events, canvassing, and direct mail) in this manual.

Exercise:
Problem 1
— Defining Your "Community"

Frequently, citizen groups define their "community" too narrowly, seeking support only from people who are directly affected by an issue, such as women office workers or senior citizens. Some groups define "community" to include all residents within a geographic boundary without considering the particular needs or interests of different types of people. This activity will help you clarify who your community is and how they might support your organization.

The Process:

1. Select a discussion leader and transfer the chart included here onto newsprint, using one sheet for each "type" of person indicated in the chart ("Potential Supporters in the Community").

2. Brainstorm responses to Columns 1, 2 and 3 for each item. Column 2, "Why They Might Be Interested In Your Organization," might be the most difficult to do; put yourself in each "type" of person's shoes and imagine how they might view your organization.

3. Compare Column 3, "What Could They Contribute to Your Organization," with a prioritized list of your organization's needs. Plan strategies for approaching each person or group of people. Assign tasks to individuals or committees to follow through with the strategies.

	Column 1	Column 2	Column 3
Potential Supporters in the Community	*Who AreThey? (names, locations, and/or characteristics)*	*Why Might They Be Interested In Your Organization?*	*What Could They Contribute To Your Organization?*

Members of your group or potential program participants

People who are sympathetic:

- locally
- in the state
- in the region
- nationwide

Institutions:

- businesses
- municipal offices
- churches
- social service agencies
- hospitals
- schools
- other community groups
- media

Influential people:

- political leaders
- bankers
- church leaders

Community residents:

- in a particular area
- income
- ethnic groups
- sex
- age
- occupation
- political ideology

Other:

There are three kinds of community leaders — people in formal leadership positions (politicians, city or county administrators, police), people who control resources (property owners, bankers, business owners), and people who hold informal leadership positions (church leaders, active community members). While you probably know who supports your group and who doesn't, it's helpful to look again for those whose support and contributions are critical to the success of a project.

Discussion Questions:

- *Discuss the kind of support your group needs from people whose names have been checked and from those who already support the project. Is it financial support, public endorsement, involvement in your activities, specific resources, access to the media and other community leaders?*

- *Discuss strategies for enlisting these people's support — paying personal visits, calling them, asking them for money, asking them to speak at one of your meetings, or sending them your newsletter.*

- *Will the strategies and activities of the group need to be altered in order to get the support of these individuals? A discussion of the risks of being co-opted is necessary before attempts are made to solicit support.*

Exercise:
Problem 2
– Failing to Get Support from Community Leaders

The Process:

1. Select a discussion leader.

2. Transfer the diagram below to newsprint and tape each sheet to a wall, side-by-side, so everyone can see them.

Leaders In The Community (Names)	Leaders Who Support The Project	Leaders Who Are Neutral About The Project	Leaders Who Oppose The Project

3. Beginning with the left-hand column, ask everyone to call out the names of people, advising participants not to dispute the suggestions at this point. Record each name on the sheet of paper.

4. When the list looks exhaustive, go back through the names, asking if everyone agrees that that person should be considered a leader in the community. If some disagree, probe for clarification and come to consensus.

5. Again, go back over the names and ask which of the three categories each person belongs in: Those who are supporters, those who are neutral, or those who oppose the project. Beside each person's name, put a check in the appropriate column. To avoid being arbitrary or hasty, the discussion leader may want to ask, "In what ways has the person helped or hindered our project?"

6. Now, look over the names in each of the three columns. Discuss which people are needed for providing support and in what ways (financial or otherwise). Put an asterisk (*) beside each person whose support is critical.

Exercise: Problem 3 — Being Shy about Asking for Donations

Because asking for money can be difficult and nerve-wracking, citizen groups often pass up opportunities to solicit donations, whether attending the annual pot-luck supper or while speaking to the local church about your organization. This is a quick activity to help you practice asking for money.

The Process:

1. Select a discussion leader.

2. Divide the group into pairs by counting off A, B, A, B, etc. For the first round, the A's are the donors and the B's are the donees.

3. The donees have five minutes to ask for money from the donor. Funds may be requested for a program, activity or any whim whatsoever.

4. Switch roles, making the A's the donees and the B's the donors, and ask for money.

5. The discussion leader should bring the group back together, asking for reactions to the exercise. Record specific suggestions about what seemed to be effective and what wasn't.

Step 6: Researching Possible Funding Sources

"Who gives money to *(day care, homeless elephants, community health centers, etc.)*?" tops the list of the 10 most popular questions about fund-raising. Unless you're conversing with a computer, the response may include a few suggestions but it's unlikely you'll get the whole spectrum of possibilities. Refer to the chapters on government, foundations and corporations for an in-depth explanation of the research process. A brief section is included here as a summary of information/resource places in Massachusetts and the most helpful research publications. Those in other states can use this as a model of what to look for in your own area.

Dist. Field Newspaper Syndicate, 1977.

Where to Find Information on Funding Sources

The following identifies key information centers in Massachusetts that can offer some assistance to the grant-seeker. In addition to visiting these resource centers, the reader is encouraged to talk with other fundraisers to learn more about fund-raising strategies and share experiences. Also listed are the most helpful publications for each topic area.

Government Sources

Information Resource Centers

Federal and state agencies: Check through the **Catalog of Federal Domestic Assistance,** the **U.S. Government Manual,** and the listing of state agencies in the Boston telephone directory. Contact those agencies that appear to be most appropriate for your organization.

Federal Bookstore, John F. Kennedy Federal Building, Boston

State Bookstore, Room 116, State House, Boston 02133

Local public and university libraries: Reference departments may have selected publications, such as the **Catalog of Federal Domestic Assistance,** the **Federal Register,** etc.

Office of Federal/State Resources, Room 527, State House, Boston, (617) 727-4178, 727-2090. Will respond to general inquiries.

Center for Community Economic Development, 639 Massachusetts Avenue, Cambridge: Has small research library on economic development, community development corporations, venture capital, etc.

Selected Research Publications

Catalog of Federal Domestic Assistance. Office of Management and Budget (Government Printing Office, Washington, D.C. 20402, $18/year). An annual publication of federal grant programs, the **Catalog** includes a general description of each program. This is the basic research tool in locating federal dollars. Details for each grant program may be requested from the appropriate federal agency.

Federal Register (Government Printing Office, $50/year). Published weekdays; contains all proposed and final regulations for federal assistance programs, including application deadlines. Updates the information in the **Catalog of Federal Domestic Assistance.**

Commerce Business Daily, U.S. Department of Commerce (Government Printing Office, $75/year). Published weekdays; contains information on current **contract** opportunities. The first part, "Services," is the most relevant for nonprofit groups, particulary Section A (Experimental, Developmental, Test and Research Work), Section H (Expert and Consultant Services), and Section U (Training).

U.S. Government Manual, Office of Federal Register (Government Printing Office, $6.50/year). Pub-

lished annually; covers each branch of government, including names of key personnel and telephone numbers. An organization chart for each federal agency is useful in understanding the structure of complex agencies such as the Department of Health, Education and Welfare.

Foundations

Information Resource Centers

Foundation Center, 888 Seventh Avenue, New York NY 10019 (212) 975-1120. Their libraries in New York, Washington, and Chicago have information on all 26,000 foundations in the U.S. and are open weekdays to the public. The Center also publishes the **Foundation Directory, Foundation Grants Index, Foundation Center Source Book Profiles** and other foundation-related materials.

Associated Foundation of Greater Boston, 294 Washington Street, Boston, MA 02108 (617) 426-2608. This regional foundation collection has information on all Massachusetts foundations and selected national foundations. Open weekdays, first-time users should call for an appointment to attend an orientation session. The most comprehensive collection in Massachusetts.

Boston Public Library, Humanities Reference Department, Copley Square, Boston, MA (617) 536-5400 ext. 531. Has information on all foundations located in New England and selected national foundations.

Hartford Public Library, 500 Main Street, Hartford, CT (203) 525-9121. This collection includes information on foundations in Massachusetts, Connecticut, Rhode Island and selected national foundations. The two collections in Boston are superior to this one in staffing, number of microfilm readers and availability of materials.

Haymarket Drop-In Center, 120 Boylston Street, Boston, MA (617) 426-1909. A small funding library concentrating on funding for social change groups.

Mass. Attorney General's Office, Charitable Trust Division, 1 Ashburton Place, 18th floor, Boston, MA (617) 727-2235. Has Mass. foundation **state** tax returns (Form 12) on file. Should be used as a backup to information centers above since the Form 12s are frequently incomplete or missing. They're now trying to change the form and make more information available to the public.

Campaign for Human Development, Chancery Annex, 73 Chestnut Street, Springfield, MA (413) 732-3175, Sister Rhonda Meister. Has a new, small funding library concentrating on funding for social change groups.

Selected Research Publications

The Foundation Directory, Edition 6, prepared by The Foundation Center (Columbia University Press, 136 South Broadway, Irving-

ton, NY 10533, $35). The most widely used directory of foundations, listing the largest 2,818 foundations. Information includes foundation address, phone number, trustees, brief statement of purpose, assets, and total grants. Further research will be needed to determine foundation program priorities, past grants and application procedures.

Foundation Grants Index, prepared by The Foundation Center (Columbia University Press, $20). Cumulative listing of grants included in the six issues of **Foundation News** for the year of publication. Published annually.

Foundation News (Council on Foundations, Box 783, Old Chelsea Station, New York, NY 10011 $20/year). Published bimonthly; contains an insert listing **current** grants of a limited number of foundations as well as articles on all aspects of foundation giving.

Directory of Foundations In Massachusetts, compiled by the Mass. Attorney General's Office (by mail from UMass Press, Box 429, Amherst, MA 01002 or in person at Associated Foundation, $7.50). Based on questions mailed to the foundations and state financial reports; includes 1,100 Massachusetts foundations.

Network of Change Oriented Foundations (Playboy Foundation, 919 North Michigan Avenue, Chicago, IL 60611, $3). A directory of basic information on 36 foundations which fund social change projects.

Foundation Center Source Book Profiles (Foundation Center, 888 Seventh Avenue, New York, NY 10019, $150). Easy to use, com-

plete information on 500 large, primarily national foundations. Includes an analysis of the foundation's grants and representative grants. May be used at the Foundation Center or regional collections.

Internal Revenue Service Private Foundation Tax Returns (990-PF and 990-AR). Copies of foundation tax returns may be ordered from IRS or may be used at The Foundation Center, Associated Foundation, Boston Public Library and Hartford Public Library. These tax returns are a primary source of information for those foundations that do not publish annual reports. The most important features of the 990s are the listing of grants paid and the foundation's telephone number.

Corporations

Information Resource Centers

Public and university libraries: Reference Departments usually have the major publications listed below.

Kirstein Library, Business Branch of Boston Public Library, 20 City Hall Avenue, Boston, MA (617) 523-0860. Extensive information on corporations.

Selected Research Publications

Standard and Poor's **Register of Corporations, Directors and Executives** (Standard and Poor, 345 Hudson Street, New York, NY, $150/year). Includes corporate addresses, telephone number, officers, directors and description of products. Entries for corporate executives include age, education, home address, and other corporate affiliations.

Dun and Bradstreet's **Million Dollar Directory** and **Middle Market Directory** (99 Church Street, New York, NY 10007, $150/year). Similar to Standard and Poor's **Register,** the various indices enable the reader to locate corporations geographically and by product classification.

Who's Who In America (Marquis Academic Media, 200 East Ohio Street, Chicago, IL 61611). An invaluable tool in gathering background information on corporate executives and prominent individuals.

Official Summary of Security Transactions and Holdings, compiled by the Securities and Exchange Commission (Government Printing Office). All officers, directors and holders of 5% or more stock in a publicly held corporation must report his/her holdings and changes (sales and purchases) to the SEC. These changes are included in this monthly publication, available in some of the larger public and university libraries.

See also: **Business Week, Fortune Magazine, Wall Street Journal, Business and Society Review** (periodicals)

Selected Materials on Fund-Raising

The Bread Game: The Realities of Foundation Funding (Glide Publications, 330 Ellis Street, San Francisco, CA 94102, $2.95). A short, informative book on raising money from foundations.

County and City Data Book (Government Printing Office, $18.65). Statistical information about U.S. counties and cities. Useful for preparing a "needs statement" for funding proposals.

Developing Skills in Proposal Writing by Mary Hall (Continuing Education Publications, 1633 S.W. Park, Portland, Oregon 97207, $10). A good guide to proposal-writing, with examples and worksheets.

Fundraising in the Public Interest, by David L. Grubb and David R. Zwick (The Public Citizen, Inc., 1346 Connecticut Avenue, N.W., Washington, D.C. 20036, $4.50) Focuses on direct mail and canvassing with sample mailers.

Grants: How to Find Out About Them and What To Do Next, by Virginia White (Plenum Press, 227 West 17th Street, New York, NY 10011, $19.50). A good overview of identifying potential funding

sources and developing a fund-raising strategy.

The Grantsmanship Center News (1015 West Olympic Boulevard, Los Angeles, CA 90015, $15/year). The best periodical on program planning, all phases of grantsmanship; filled with "how to" articles.

The Grassroots Fundraising Book, by Joan Flanagan (Swallow Press, P.O. Box 988, Hicksville, NY 18802, $5.25). Everything you need to know to plan fund-raising events. An exciting book loaded with ideas, cautions, checklists and a process for planning an annual calendar of events.

Handbook of Special Events for Nonprofit Organizations, by Edwin Liebert and Bernice Sheldon (Association Press). A good overview of planning large fund-raising events.

The Rich and the Super-rich, by Ferdinand Lundberg (Bantam Books, $2.25). A well-documented analysis of who owns America.

Reprinted from Workforce

Frequently Asked Questions about the Research Process

1. **Who Should Do This Kind of Research?**

    Fundraisers often attempt to take on the research task alone. As a result, most fundraisers have drooping shoulders from carrying hefty volumes; they may start to see double images (mostly numbers) and daydream for diversion. In spite of these conditions, some fundraisers prefer to work alone because it permits them to be consistent in collecting funding information.

    Another option is to involve several people — some researching government funding, some covering corporations, individuals and foundations and still others planning a series of fundraising events. The *advantage* is that more people will learn how to do the research and it can be completed in a fewer number of days. The *danger* is that each person will select possible funding sources based on different criteria. One possible solution is for the fundraiser to go with volunteers the first time, explaining the research process *at the information center.*

2. **Are There Any Shortcuts?**

    There are some organizations that offer computer search services to nonprofit organizations, but the database (information stored in the computer) is often incomplete and expensive to use. Here are some questions to ask organizations that offer this service:

    - How much will it cost? How is the price determined?

    - Is the information in the database complete (e.g. does it cover all 26,000 foundations or just the largest)?

    - How current is the information?

    - What kind of information will I get? (Ask for a sample printout.)

    - Could I have the names of other people who have used this service?

    In general, computer search services are an expensive way to compile information that is readily accessible.

3. **How Thorough Should the Research Be?**

    If your organization has decided to seek outside funding, then you have immediately placed yourselves in competition with many other organizations. Therefore, the more "homework" that's done, the better off you'll be. The best research is that which can be used by everyone in the organization, which means permanent files, a simple filing system, and easy-to-read forms. When the person responsible for doing the fund-raising leaves the organization, the next person will have an easier time picking up where (s)he left off.

    Profile sheets similar to the following may be used for each potential funding source, possibly supplemented with a card file.

30

Corporation Profile Sheet

Name of corporation:_____

Address:_____Telephone:_____

_____

Type of business (products):_____

_____

Annual Sales: $_____   Number of employees:_____

Profits: 197_: $_____   197_: $_____

         198_: $_____   198_: $_____

Board of Directors: Stockholdings of Directors:

_____   _____

_____   _____

_____   _____

_____   _____

_____   _____

_____   _____

_____   _____

_____   _____

Officers: Stockholdings and Salaries:

_____   _____

_____   _____

_____   _____

_____   _____

_____   _____

_____   _____

_____   _____

_____   _____

_____   _____

Members of Corporate Gifts Committee:_____

_____

_____

Major Shareholders:_____

_____

_____

Subsidiary Companies:_____

_____

_____

_____

_____

Location of Branch Offices or Factories:_____

_____

_____

_____

_____

_____

_____

Known Contributions to Other Nonprofit Organizations:_____

_____

_____

_____

_____

_____

_____

_____

_____

Connection with Our Organization:_____

_____

_____

Previous Donations to Our Organization:_____

_____

_____

_____

Comments:

32

Individual Profile Sheet

Name:_____

Home Address:_____   Telephone:_____
_____

Occupation:_____

Business Address:_____   Telephone: _____
_____

Previous Employers:_____
_____
_____

Corporate Directorships: _____
_____
_____

Political Offices Held:_____
_____

Other Affiliations (clubs, nonprofit board memberships):_____
_____
_____
_____

Share Holdings (at market value):_____
_____
_____
_____

Education:_____
Family members (spouse, children):_____
_____

Known contributions to Nonprofit Organizations:_____
_____
_____
_____

Connection with Our Organization:_____
_____

Previous Donations to Our Organization:_____
_____
_____

Comments:

Foundation Profile Sheet

Fiscal Year Ending _____

Telephone _____

Foundation Name _____

Address _____

President _____

Vice-President _____

Treasurer _____

Secretary _____

Director _____

Trustees _____

_____

_____

_____

_____

_____

Assets: Market Value _____   Book Value _____

Liabilities _____   Net Worth _____

Gifts Received _____   Source _____

Foundation Donor(s) _____

Date of Exemption _____   Meeting Dates _____

Purpose _____

Restrictions _____

_____

Total Grants _____   Number of Grants _____

Average Grant/Range _____

Type of Grants (operating, etc.) _____

Background Information on Trustees _____

_____

_____

_____

_____

_____

_____

Comments

Staff

34

Foundation Name _____

Address _____

Grants _____

_____

_____

_____

_____

_____

_____

_____

_____

_____

_____

_____

_____

_____

_____

_____

_____

_____

_____

_____

_____

_____

_____

_____

_____

_____

_____

_____

_____

_____

_____

_____

_____

_____

_____

_____

Step 7:
Prioritizing Possible Funding Sources

Even if you've uncovered only two possible funding sources during your search, you might wonder which one to concentrate on first. Frequently, a fundraiser is expected to explore all possibilities. This can lead to a schizophrenic scramble to get it all done. Ranking your list of funding sources clears up some of the bewilderment and pressure.

Suggested follow-up:

Those funding sources with the lowest scores are the ones on which the fundraiser should concentrate. A discussion following the score tally could focus on checking for consensus among the group members and talking about the implications of the final choice.

The Process:

1. The fundraiser should pass out completed profile sheets for each prospective donor and briefly summarize her/his impressions of each possible funding source. It's assumed that the fundraiser will be the discussion leader for this activity.

2. Allowing time for questions, the fundraiser should distribute copies of the Rating Sheet with the first column already completed.

3. Working individually, each person should spend a minimum of three minutes per funding source, ranking them from 1-10 for each criteria (1 = Best Bet, 10 = Worst Bet).

4. When each person is finished, ask them to total their scores in the Individual Total Score column.

5. Total all the individual scores in the Group Total Score column.

FUNDING SOURCE RANKING SHEET

Rank each funding source from 1-10 (1 = Best Bet, 10 = Worst Bet)

Name of funding source	How closely does this funding source match our program and philosophy?	Will funding from this source help meet our most critical need?	Realistically, do we have a chance of getting funding from this source?	Is the time and cost required to get funds worth the anticipated level of funding?	Individual Total Score	Total Group Score
1.						
2.						
3.						
4.						
5.						
6.						
7.						
8.						

Exercise:
Preparing a Funding Timetable

Even after possible funding sources are ranked, there is still the risk of losing a few in the shuffle or concentrating on one or two and doing nothing about the others. A detailed timetable can help organize your funding strategy into task completion deadlines. It's also a good way to keep everyone informed about the status of the fund-raising activities.

Suggested follow-up:

The use of index cards is suggested because they can easily be removed and updated with current information. Another option is a roll of adding machine tape attached horizontally to the wall.

In order to keep the timetable updated and check on your group's progress, you may want to refer to it during staff meetings, asking the person responsible for each task to give a brief statement about their progress. If deadlines are missed, then the group should decide whether or not to change the deadline or add more people to the task. This serves as an accountability mechanism as well.

The Process:

1. On 3 x 5 index cards, write the name of each month of the year and tape the cards across a wall in a horizontal line.

2. Write the name of each possible funding source on an index card and tape them to the wall in a vertical line, according to their priority ranking.

3. Brainstorm all of the tasks that need to be completed for each funding source and assign completion deadlines for each task.

4. Tape a horizontal line of blank index cards for each funding source.

5. On each horizontal track, put a slash (/) at the beginning and end of the projected "activity period," and connect the two slashes with a horizontal line.

6. Indicate specific task deadlines for each track under the appropriate months.

(See the sample timetable included in this exercise for a better idea of how to do it.)

Sample Funding Timetable

	Jan. 1978	Feb.	Mar.	Apr.	May	June	July	Aug.	Sept.	Oct.	Nov.	Dec.
Fund-raising event: Spaghetti Supper	Form committee / Prepare budget / Set ticket price / Set date	Find space / Recruit workers / Print & distribute tickets & posters	Publicize event / Supper / Prepare food / Set up space	Clean-up / Thank-yous to workers								
Megabucks Foundation			Completed research / Phone call	Submit concept paper / Meet with fdn. staff	Submit final proposal	Begin negotiating			Final decision / Write thank-you			

38

Step 8:
Making the Initial Contact with the Funding Source

Once you've identified appropriate funding sources for your organization and have gathered all the written information available on them, then comes the question of how to approach the funding source. The four basic options are (1) a personal visit to the funding source, (2) a telephone call, (3) a brief letter describing the organization and program, and (4) a proposal outlining all the details of the program. Although there are no hard-and-fast rules, you could consider the following criteria in determining how you will approach the funding source:

- **Whether or not the funding source has staff people to help you.** Government agencies, some large national foundations, some corporations, and national church offices have hired staff people to handle many of their grant-making responsibilities. If you think the funding source has staff, phone calls requesting *specific* information (application procedures, proposal deadlines, etc.) are appropriate. Government agencies, in particular, are usually more than willing to spend time talking with prospective applicants, either on the phone or in person.

Funding sources without staff, especially small foundations and corporations, are not likely to respond well to telephone inquiries. The best strategy is to submit a brief proposal (10 pages) and follow it up with a phone call a few weeks later.

- **How the funding source operates.** Some funding sources have application procedures that are described in their written materials. You could also contact an organization that has received funding in the past and ask for their impression of how the funding source operates.

- **Your personal style.** Do you feel comfortable talking on the telephone? Is it easier for you to write a brief letter and follow it up with a phone call?

- **What do you want the first contact to accomplish?** Be clear about your intended results of the initial contact. One mistake that many groups make is to ask general questions which indicate that they have not done their homework. Are you seeking information, scheduling an appointment, letting them know that an application is on the way, asking for clarification of a question on the application form, or a combination of the above?

One strategy that appears to be the least successful is to call a funding source, describe the project, and ask if it sound appropriate to submit a proposal. In most cases, the person will respond negatively, either because (s)he doesn't want to be bothered with another proposal or because (s)he is asked to make a snap decision with very little information about the project.

Exercise:
Initial Phone Call to a Funding Sources (Role-Play)

One of the best ways to prepare for the first contact with a funding source is to practice. This activity focuses on the phone calling process since that is the usual route for applications for federal, large corporate and national foundation funding.

The Process:

1. Review your list of possible funding sources and decide which type you'll concentrate on first (government, corporate, foundation, church, or other).

2. Pair off and decide which person is the fundraiser and which is the potential donor. During the role-play, the fundraiser should use details from an actual project.

3. Both "grantor" and "applicant" should look over the suggested questions and responses and select those which are appropriate for the situation, adding others as needed.

4. The "applicant" calls the "funding source." This can be done by placing two chairs back-to-back, or by actually placing a telephone call.

5. In pairs, discuss how the phone call went. The "grantor" should be prepared to make suggestions about improving the presentation.

6. Switch roles, if desired, and repeat the steps above.

7. If more than one pair is doing the activity, end the role-play with a discussion of specific problems that each pair had and suggestions about what strategies worked.

Possible Questions and Responses for the Role-Play

Fundraiser: Possible Questions	Corporate Funding Source: Possible Responses	Foundation Funding Source: Possible Responses
• May I talk with the person who's responsible for (*corporate gifts, XYZ federal assistance program, foundation funding, etc.*)? • What is the application process? • What are the proposal deadlines? • Do you have any information you could send me? • Do you have specific proposal requirements (length, content, forms)? • When will funding decisions be made? • To whom should the proposal be submitted? • Would you like me to send you a two or three page letter describing the project or a longer proposal? • I'd like to schedule an appointment to talk with you about our programs. When would that be convenient?	• I'm sorry, we don't give grants to community groups. • I'm sorry, we can only consider proposals from groups working in ABC Community. • Let me connect you with Paula Public Relations. • I'm sorry, all our community funds are committed for this year. • I'll send you some information about the application process. • Send in your proposal and I'll get back to you in a few months. **Government Funding Source: Possible Responses** • What is the **CFDA (Catalog of Federal Domestic Assistance)** number of the program you're calling about? • I'll send you a packet of information, including an application form. • Funds haven't yet been appropriated for this program. • I'll be happy to meet with you. When are you coming to Washington? • What specific questions do you have about the program?	• The trustees have not scheduled their next meeting. • (*If a national foundation*): Send in a brief letter describing the project. If it is consistent with our funding priorities, you will be requested to submit a full proposal. • (*If a small foundation*): We cannot meet with applicants because it takes too much time. Funding decisions are based on written proposals. • (*If a large foundation*): We would be happy to meet with you once your proposal has been reviewed. • We don't supply application forms. Send us a 10 - 15 page proposal. (*Note: This usually the case with a small foundation; most national foundations don't have application forms, but proposals are generally longer.*) • (*If a small foundation*): Our funds are non-discretionary, which means that they are paid to the same organizations every year. • We have no funds left to distribute until next year.

Step 9: Writing and Editing Proposals

Proposal writing is an art that requires good writing skills, logic and practice. Readers are encouraged to go through *Program Planning and Proposal Writing* (an article prepared by the Grantsmanship Center) which appears in this section and refer to the books listed under *Resources*.

The two activities in this section concentrate on reviewing proposals. By actually critiquing proposals that others have written, participants in these exercises can learn more about techniques for writing their own.

THE WORKBOOK /cpf

Drawing by Aubrey Beardsley

PROGRAM PLANNING & PROPOSAL WRITING

By Norton J. Kiritz
Executive Director
THE GRANTSMANSHIP CENTER®
© Copyright

Proposals written for foundations and those written for federal grants will differ markedly in final form. Foundations usually require a brief letter; federal agencies usually require you to complete an extensive array of forms and possibly attach your own narrative.

We suggest the following format as a basic planning format for all proposals. Thinking through the various sections as we suggest will enable you to draw from the content virtually all that either a private or public funding source will ask from you. Thinking through the various components will also enable you to develop a logical way to approach your plans and programs. And hopefully this planning will make your programs more effective.

The proposal format looks like this:

Proposal Summary
I Introduction
II Problem Statement or Assessment of Need
III Program Objectives
IV Methods
V Evaluation
VI Future Funding
VII Budget

Proposal Summary

The summary is a very important part of a proposal — not just something you jot down as an afterthought. There may be a box for a summary on the first page of a federal grant application form. In writing to a foundation, the summary may be presented as a cover letter, or the first paragraph of a letter-type proposal. The summary is probably the first thing that a funding source will read. It should be clear, concise and specific. It should describe who you are, the scope of your project, and the projected cost.

Some funding sources may screen proposals as a first step in grant-making. That is, they briefly examine each proposal to see if it is consistent with their priorities, if it is from an agency eligible to apply for their funds, etc. As a further step, the "screeners" may draw up a summary of their own and these proposal summaries may be all that is reviewed in the next step of the process. It is much better to spend the time to draw up a summary of your own that the funding source can use than to hope that the reviewer sees the importance of your program in his brief initial look at your proposal. So do a good job!

I
Introduction

This is the section of a proposal where you tell who you are. Many proposals tell little or nothing about the applicant organization and speak only about the project or program to be conducted. More often than not proposals are funded on the basis of the reputation or "connections" of the applicant organization or its key personnel rather than on the basis of the program's content alone. The Introduction is the section in which you build your credibility as an organization which should be supported.

Credibility

What gives an organization credibility in the eyes of a funding source? Well, first of all, it depends on the funding source. A traditional, rather conservative funding source will be more responsive to persons of prominence on your Board of Directors, how long you have been in existence, how many other funding sources have been supporting you, and other similar characteristics of your organization. An "avant garde" funding source might be more interested in a Board of "community persons" rather than of prominent citizens and in organizations that are new rather than established, etc.

Potential funding sources should be selected because of their possible interest in your type of organization or your type of program. You can use the introduction to reinforce the connection you see between your interests and those of the funding source.

What are some of the things you can say about your organization in an introductory section?

- How you got started.

- How long you have been around.

- Anything unique about the way you got started, or the fact that you were the first thus-and-so organization in the country, etc.

- Some of your most significant accomplishments as an organization or, if you are a new organization, some of the significant accomplishments of your Board or staff in their previous roles.

- Your organizational goals — why you were started.

- What support you have received from other organizations and prominent individuals (accompanied by some letters of endorsement which can be in an appendix).

We strongly suggest that you start a "credibility file" which you can use as a basis for the introductory section of future proposals you write. In this file you can keep copies of newspaper articles about your organization, letters of support you receive from other agencies and from your clients. Include statements made by key figures in your field or in the political arena that endorse your kind of program even if they do not mention your agency.

For example, by including a presidential commission's statement that the type of program which you are proposing has the most potential of solving the problems with which you deal, you can borrow credibility from those who made the statement (if they have any).

Remember, the credibility you establish in your introduction may be more important than the rest of your proposal. Build it! But here, as in all of your proposal, be as brief and specific as you can. Avoid jargon and keep it simple.

II
Problem Statement or Assessment of Need

In the introduction you have told who you are. From the introduction we should now know your areas of interest — the field in which you are working. Now you will zero in on the specific problem or problems that you want to solve through the program you are proposing.

Pitfalls

There are some common pitfalls which agencies face when they try to define problems.

Sometimes an organization will paint a broad picture of all the ills plaguing people in a part of the community. Proposal writers do not narrow down to a specific problem or problems that are solvable, and they leave the funding source feeling that it will take a hundred times the requested budget even to begin to deal with the problems identified. This is overkill. It often comes from the conviction of the applicant that it must draw a picture of a needy community in all its dimensions in order to convince the funding source that there are really problems there. All that this does is to leave the funding source asking: "How can this agency possibly hope to deal with all of those problems." Don't overkill.

Narrow down your definition of the problem you want to deal with to something you can hope to accomplish within a reasonable amount of time and with reasonable additional resources.

Document the Problem

Document the problem. How do you know that a problem really exists? Don't just assume that "everybody knows this is a problem...." That may be true, but it doesn't give a funding source any assurance about your capabilities if you fail to demonstrate your knowledge of the problem. You should use some key statistics here. Don't fill your proposal with tables, charts and graphs. They will probably turn off the reader. If you must use extensive statistics, save them for an appendix, but pull out the key figures for your problem statement. And know what the statistics say.

We saw one proposal where an agency presented demographic (population statistics) pictures of two communities, one in which the program was to be conducted and another nearby community where there would not be a program. Every statistic (percentage unemployment, ethnic breakdown, number of youth, number of juvenile arrests, etc.) pointed to a vastly greater problem in Community B than Community A yet Community A was the proposed site of the new program. Any reviewer would seriously question the program based on those accompanying statistics.

To summarize, you need to do the following:

- Make a logical connection between your organization's background and the problems and needs with which you propose to work.

- Support the existence of the problem by evidence. Statistics, as mentioned above, are but one type of support. You may also get advice from groups in your community concerned about the problem, from prospective clients, and from other organizations working in your community and professionals in the field.

- Define clearly the problems with which you intend to work. Make sure that what you want to do is workable — that it can be done within a reasonable time, by you, and with a reasonable amount of money.

III
Program Objectives

One of your concerns throughout your proposal should be to develop a logical flow from one section to another. Whereas you can use your introduction to set the context for your problem statement, you can likewise use the problem statement to prepare the funding source for your objectives.

An objective is a specific, measurable outcome of your program.

Clearly, if you have defined a problem, then your objectives should offer some relief of the problem. If the problem which you identify is a high incidence of drug abuse by youth in your community (substantiated, of course), then an objective of your program should be the reduction of the incidence of drug abuse among youth in your community. If the problem is unemployment, then an objective is the reduction of unemployment.

Distinguish between
Methods and Objectives

One common problem in many proposals is a failure to distinguish between means and ends — a failure to distinguish between methods and objectives.

For example, many proposals read like this:

"The purpose of this proposal is to establish a peer-group tutoring program for potential drop-outs in the _____ area of Los Angeles," or

"The objective of this program is to provide counseling and guidance services for delinquent youth in _____."

What's wrong with these objectives? They don't speak about outcome! If I support your project for a year, or for two years, and come back at that time and say, "I want to see what you have done—what you have accomplished," what can you tell me? The fact that you have established a service, or conducted some activities, doesn't tell me whether you have helped to solve the problem which you defined. I want to know what you have accomplished. I want to know the outcome of your activities. I want to know whether you have, through your tutoring program, reduced the number of drop-outs with whom you have worked, or whether the delinquent youth with whom you worked got into less trouble over the past year. Knowing that you worked at it is not enough!

Some organizations, trying to be as specific as they can, pick a number out of the air as their measurable objective. For example, an agency might say that their objective is to "decrease unemployment among adults in the XYZ community by 10 percent." The question I ask is where did they get that figure? Usually it is made up because it sounds good. It sounds like a real achievement. But it should be made of something more substantial than that. Perhaps no program has ever achieved that high a percentage. Perhaps similar programs have resulted in a range of achievement of from 2 to 6 percent decrease in unemployment. In that case, 5 percent would be very good, and 6 percent would be as good as ever has been done. Ten percent is just plain unrealistic. And it leads me to expect that you don't really know the field very well.

If you are having difficulty in defining your objectives, try projecting your agency a year or two into the future. What differences would you hope to see between then and now? What changes would have occurred? These changed dimensions may be the objectives of your program.

In addition, I want to examine your objectives in a little more detail. Maybe some programs create jobs for people that are very temporary in nature, and they reduce the unemployment problem in the short term, but after a year or two the problem will be back with us, as bad, or worse, than ever. This gets into the question of evaluation, which clearly relates to the setting of measurable objectives — for a good set of well-drawn and realistic objectives becomes a set of criteria for the evaluation of the program and thus serves another purpose.

IV
Methods

By now you have told me who you are, the problem(s) you want to work with, and your objectives (which promise a solution to or reduction of the problems), and now you are going to tell me how you will bring about these results. You will describe the methods you will use — the activities you will conduct to accomplish your objectives.

Research

The informed reviewer wants to know why you have selected these methods. Why do you think they will work? This requires you to know a good deal about other programs of a similar nature. Who is working on the problem in your community and elsewhere? What methods have been tried in the past and are being tried now and with what results? In other words, can you substantiate your choice of methods?

One agency recently brought a proposal into class that dealt with the provision of counseling services to delinquent youth by professional social workers with MSW degrees. Each of these two professional staff members was to receive a salary in excess of $15,000 per year. The agency was concerned about the limited number of MSW's they could hire within their budget limitations.

A number of questions were raised about this program. One key question was this — why did you decide that professional social workers with MSW degrees and $15,000 salaries were necessary to the success of your program? Do you have any evidence that similar programs have been effective elsewhere? What other models exist that you could work with? Is it possible that para-professionals (non-degreed workers, even ex-offenders themselves) could do the job as well as or perhaps better than the trained professionals you want to hire? Do you know of programs using para-professionals in this capacity and have you assessed the results of such programs? How can you complain of lack of sufficient money to employ more than these two highly-trained staff when you don't know if there is a less expensive, and perhaps more successful, model to follow.

The consideration of alternatives is an important aspect of describing your methodology. Showing that you are familiar enough about your field to be aware of different models for solving the problems, and showing your reasons for selecting the model that you have, gives a funding source a feeling of security that you know what you are doing, and adds greatly to your credibility.

One planning technique which you might want to use is this. Take a sheet of paper and divide it into columns. The first column is the "problem" column, the second is headed "objectives," the third "methods" and the fourth "evaluation." If you list all your objectives separately in the second column, you can then identify the problem that it relates to, the specific methods in your program that deal with the objective, and the criteria of success in reaching the objective as well as the method of evaluation.

This helps you to see whether you are truly dealing with all of the problems you talked about, whether your objectives relate to the problem(s), whether you have a method of reaching each objective, and whether you have set up an evaluation mechanism to deal with your entire program. This leads us into the next proposal component — evaluation.

V Evaluation

Evaluation of your program can serve two purposes for your organization. Your program can be evaluated in order to determine how effective it is in reaching the objectives you have established -- in solving the problems you are dealing with. This concept of evaluation is geared towards the results of your program.

Evaluation can also be used as a tool to provide information necessary to make appropriate changes and adjustments in your program as it proceeds.

As we have stated, measurable objectives set the stage for an effective evaluation. If you have difficulty in determining what criteria to use in evaluating your program, better take another look at your objectives. They probably aren't very specific.

Subjective and Objective Evaluations

Also, be sure you understand the difference between subjective and objective evaluations.

Subjective evaluations of programs are rarely evaluations at all. They may tell you about how people feel about a program, but seldom deal with the concrete results of a program. For example, we saw an example of an evaluation of an educational program that surveyed opinions about program success held by students, parents, teachers and administrators of the program. This is a pretty "soft" evaluation, and doesn't really give much evidence to support the tangible results of such a program.

In addition, this particular evaluation solicited comments from students when they completed the program, failing to deal with over 50 percent of the students who started but did not complete the program. Clearly, those students who finished the program are going to react differently, as a group, from those who didn't complete the program. And we might, as an agency, learn a great deal from those who didn't finish. From the nature of this evaluation, one might suppose that the educational institution involved was committed to producing what they thought would look like a good evaluation, but it wouldn't pass muster with a critical reviewer.

Subjectivity — introducing our own biases into an evaluation -- will often come in when we evaluate our own programs. Particularly if we feel that continued funding depends on producing what looks like a good evaluation.

One way of obtaining a more objective evaluation, and sometimes a more professionally prepared evaluation, is to look to an outside organization to conduct an evaluation for you. You might go to other non-profit agencies, colleges and universities in your community which will work with you in developing an evaluation for your program. Sometimes it is possible to get an outside organization to develop an evaluation design and proposal for evaluation that can be submitted to a funding source complete with its own budget, along with your proposal. This not only can guarantee a more objective evaluation, but can also add to the credibility of your total application, since you have borrowed the credibility of the evaluating institution.

It is essential to build your evaluation into your proposal and to be prepared to implement your evaluation at the same time that you start your program, or before. If you want to determine change along some dimension, then you have got to show where your clients have come from. It is very difficult to start an evaluation at or near the conclusion of a program, for you usually don't know the characteristics of the people you are working with as they existed prior to being in your program.

An Excellent
Program Evaluation

I'd like to give you an example of what I think was a very fine program evaluation. It took a lot of time and resources to conduct, and it may look like a pretty big project in and of itself. That is true. The agency that conducted this evaluation had the resources to do it. But evaluations of this nature may have enough value in and of themselves to be able to be funded quite separately and distinctly from the programs to which they are attached.

Some years ago the Los Angeles County Probation Department operated what was called the Group Guidance Program. Group Guidance was a program that employed "streetwise" Probation Officers as gang workers, with the goal of orienting gangs away from criminal behavior and into more productive activities. Some agencies questioned the effectiveness of the program and an evaluation design was created. (This is not a particularly good practice in setting up evaluations, in that evaluations set up to justify the continued existence of a program, and conducted by the agency itself, tend to be biased in favor of the agency.)

What is interesting is the evaluation design itself. It was an attempt to gather information about the presumed reduction in delinquent behavior among gang members involved in the project, and to put this data into an economic context which would justify the cost of the program. This is the basic evaluation design.

Gangs were identified which had reputations of being violent, moderate and quiet. It was proposed that the violent gangs got into far more trouble than the other two, and that this would be reflected in their court records — they would be arrested more often, would be in jail and juvenile hall more often and for longer periods of time, would spend more time at correctional facilities, etc. The Probation Department, with access to court records, examined the records of all members of these varied gangs. They identified all contacts that a youth could have with one institution or another and then went to each institution, conferred with their business department, and came away with a cost figure, in dollars and cents, that could be attached to a particular entry on a court record. In other words, it cost X dollars for a youth to spend the night in Juvenile Hall and Y dollars for 24 hours in a Probation Camp. Each gang member's record had a dollar value attached to it.

The result of this was the finding that the three kinds of gangs in question did cost the community a varying amount of money, with much higher costs being attributed to the violent gang.

The agency had done a number of things in designing this evaluation. It had established a measurable "index of delinquency" and it had created a "dollar and cents" measure which could demonstrate to the funding source, the Board of Supervisors of the County of Los Angeles, a possible saving which could be realized were the records to show that the decrease in cost for the gangs worked with in the program was greater than the cost of conducting the program itself. Pretty ingenious!

The project proceeded with the involvement of the Group Guidance worker with the most violent gang, the provision of some form of peripheral services to the moderate gang by another agency and no "treatment" at all for the quiet gang.

The evaluation was a log of further contacts by gang members with social agencies, a determination of their cost, and an examination of whether the cost of the gang worker was paid for by the reduction in recorded offenses on the part of gang members with whom he worked.

VI
Future Funding

This is the last section of your proposal, but by no means the least important. Increasingly, funding sources want to know how you will continue your program when their grant runs out. This is irrelevant for one-time only grant applications such as requests for vehicles, equipment, etc. But if you are requesting program money, if you are adding to your projects through this proposal, then how will you keep it going next year?

A promise to continue looking for alternate sources of support is not sufficient. You must present a plan that will assure the funding source, to the greatest extent possible, that you will be able to maintain this new program after their grant has been completed. They don't want to adopt you — they don't want you continually on their back for additional funds. Moreover, if you are having problems keeping your current operations supported, you will probably have much more difficulty in maintaining a level of operation which includes additional programs. The funding source may be doing you no favor by supporting a new project and putting you in the position of having to raise even more money next year than you do now.

What is a good method to guarantee continued support for a project? One good way is to get a local institution or governmental agency to agree to continue to support your program, should it demonstrate the desired results. But get such a commitment in writing. A plan to generate funds through the project itself — such as fees for services that will build up over a year or two, subscriptions to publications, etc.—is an excellent plan. The best plan for future funding is the plan that does not require outside grant support.

VII Budget

As with proposals themselves, funding source requirements for budgets differ, with foundations requiring less extensive budgets than federal agencies. The following budget design will satisfy most funding sources that allow you to design your own budget and, with minor changes that the sources will tell you about, can be adapted to fit most federal agency requirements. Our recommended budget contains two components — the first is Personnel and the second is Non-Personnel. You can expect that in most social service and related programs, approximately 80 percent of the budget will fall into the three components of the Personnel section.

I. PERSONNEL

A. Wages & Salaries

In this section you list all full and part-time staff in the proposed program. We suggest the following layout.

(No. of persons in each position)	(Title)	(Monthly salary)	(% time on project)	(No. of mos employed in grant period)	Total Requested Donated

How does this look on a completed budget? Well, if you are employing an Executive Director at a salary of $1,000 a month, working full-time (100 percent) for the entire grant period (12 months) and you are asking the funding source to provide his salary, then it looks like this:

Requested Donated

(1) Executive Director at
   $1,000 per mo. (100% time) $ 12,000
   x 12 mos.

You can list all of your staff this same way. If any of your staff are being paid out of another source of funds (for example, a staff person assigned to your project by a County agency) then you total up their salary and put it in the "donated" column. This column might also be called "non-federal" share in the case of federal programs, or also "matching" or "in-kind" contribution. Like this:

Requested Donated

(2) Counselors at $700 per mo.
   (50% time) x 6 mos. $4,200

This means that you will have two half-time counselors on your staff for six months and their salaries are being paid by somebody other than the funding source you are applying to. You still put their full-time salary in the budget ($700 per month), take half of it (they are only working 50 percent time), multiply the $350 by the six months they will be working on this project (giving you $2,100), and multiply by 2 (the number of people employed in this capacity). This

gives you a total of $4,200 of donated counselor services in this project.

What does the $1,000 per month figure for the salary of the Executive Director represent?

It may represent his or her actual salary for each month of the year. However, particularly in a new program, it may not. Our suggestion is that all organizations develop a five-step salary schedule for each job in the organization. The salary range for an Executive Director in the above agency may look like this:

Step A	Step B	Step C	Step D	Step E
$900/mo	$950/mo	$1,000/mo	$1,050/mo.	$1,100/mo.

If you have developed this kind of salary schedule for each position, then you can place in the monthly salary column of your budget the middle step of the salary range for each position, place an asterisk next to each quoted salary, and a note at the bottom of the salary section telling the reader that all salaries are listed at the middle step of the salary range for that position. Then you can attach your salary schedule to the budget. This method allows for a good deal of flexibility in fixing salaries for individuals that are hired.

For example you may have somebody in mind for the Executive Director's job who is presently earning $825 per month, and who would be delighted to come to work for you at the first step of the salary range for Executive Director ($900 per month). On the other hand, there may be an outstanding candidate for the job who is presently earning $1,000 per month, and who wouldn't come to work for you for less than $1,050 per month. Using salary range in this manner allows you to employ either person, at the appropriate salary, with the assumption being that all persons' salaries will average out towards the middle of the salary range.

How do you determine what the salary range for an Executive Director for your agency ought to be?

The federal government requires that all of your salaries are comparable to the prevailing practices in similar agencies in your community. To justify the salaries you build into your budget you must obtain information from other local agencies regarding the salaries of persons with job descriptions, qualifications and responsibilities similar to those of the jobs in your agency. You might go to the local city and/or county government, the school district, the United Way or United Fund, etc. By comparing the jobs in your agency with the jobs at other local agencies, you plan a salary for each position, and you keep the "comparability data" on hand, should you be asked by the funding source to justify your staff salaries.

B. Fringe Benefits

In this section you list all the fringe benefits your employees will be receiving, and the dollar cost of these benefits. Some fringe benefits are mandatory — but these vary from state to state, so you will have to determine what they are for your agency in your state. Mandatory fringe benefits may include State Disability Insurance, Unemployment Compensation, Retirement Contributions, etc. Most nonprofit agencies may vote, when they are started, not to participate in Social Security. These fringe benefits are all based on a percentage of salaries. For example, FICA, which is going up, has been based on 5.85 percent of the first $10,000 of each person's salary. Therefore, an entry for FICA on your budget might look like this:

	Requested	Donated
FICA at 5.85% x $87,000	$5,090	

$87,000 is the total of all your salaries, up to $10,800 for any one person.

Some fringe benefits may be paid not on a percentage of salary, but with an absolute dollar amount for each employee. For example:

	Requested	Donated
Health Insurance at $10 per mo. x 8 employees x 12 mos.	$960	

How do you determine what fringe benefits to provide to employees in your agency?

If you already operate a variety of programs your answer is simple. Employees in a new project receive the same fringe benefits as those you already employ in some other activity. The federal government requires this parity, and it is a good practice. If you are starting a new agency, or haven't formulated a fringe benefit policy yet, then you go to the same kinds of figures as you did when establishing your salary schedule — you provide in fringe benefits what is comparable to the prevailing practice in similar agencies in your community.

C. Consultants & Contract Services

This is the third and final part of the Personnel section of your budget. In this section you include paid and unpaid consultants, volunteers and services for which you contract. For example, your project may not be large enough to warrant hiring a full-time bookkeeper, and you may want to use a bookkeeping service to keep up your books. An entry in your budget will look like this:

	Requested	Donated
Bookkeeping Service at $75 per mo. x 12 mos.		

You should be running your two totals columns — requested and donated — through your entire proposal, so you have a choice of where you put the total for this service. If you are going to pay for it, it goes in the "requested" column:

	Requested	Donated
Bookkeeping Service at 75 per mo. x 12 mos.	$900	

If the services are being provided free by a friend of the project then it goes in the "donated" column:

	Requested	Donated
Bookkeeping Service at $75 per mo. x 12 mos.		$900

It is important to develop as much donated services and equipment as possible. No funding source likes to feel it is being asked to carry the entire burden of a project. If the project really means something to you and to your community, then you should have been able to develop a substantial "matching" contribution in your budget. Other kinds of contract services that might be included would be for auditing, public relations, etc.

In this section you can include all of your volunteer assistance. How do you value a volunteer's time for budgetary purposes? Well, federal agencies maintain lists of various types of jobs, and assign a value to each hour of volunteer time for each position. For example, the time of a professional Social Worker may be valued at $7.50 per hour, and would look like this in your budget:

	Requested	Donated
(1) Volunteer Social Worker at $7.50 per hr. x 4 hrs. per wk. x 40 wks.		$1,200

The figure which you get from a federal agency volunteer valuation list may be less than the actual current hourly salary of the volunteer. In that case, you may use the actual hourly salary, but be prepared to substantiate that figure. Or, the volunteer may have worked as a paid consultant for $10 per hour. You can use that figure if you can document it.

With all of your volunteers you are required to deliver the promised volunteer services, just as if the funding source was actually paying their salary, and you will be asked to document the work performed by volunteers and keep records of their volunteer time which may be audited in the case of a federal grant.

II. NON-PERSONNEL
A. Space Costs

In this section you list all of the facilities you will be using, both those on which you pay rent and those which are being donated for your use. Rent you pay, or the valuation of donated facilities, must be comparable to prevailing rents in the geographic area in which you are located. In addition to the actual rent, you should also include the cost of utilities, maintenance services and renovations, if they are absolutely essential to your program.

B. Rental, Lease or Purchase of Equipment

Here you list all of the equipment, donated or to be purchased, that will be used in the proposed program. This includes office equipment, typewriters, Xerox machines, etc. Let discretion be your guide in this section. Try to obtain as much donated equipment as you can. It not only lowers the cost of the program, but it shows the funding source that other people are involved in trying to make the program happen.

C. Consumable Supplies

This means supplies such as paper clips, paper, pens, pencils, etc. A reasonable figure to use is $75 per year for each of your staff. If you have any unusual needs for supplies — perhaps you are making a workroom available for community persons — then put in a separate figure for that. For example:

	Requested	Donated
18 staff x $75 per year	$600	
Supplies for community work-room x $30 per mo. x 12 mos.	$360	

D. Travel

Divide the section up into local and out-of-town travel. Don't put in any big lump sums which will require interpretation or raise a question at the funding source. Remember, on local mileage all of your staff won't be driving on the job, and not all who do will drive the same amount. For example:

	Requested	Donated
Out-of-town travel		
(1) Community Organizer to NACD training program in Detroit, July 5-8, $242 round-trip airfare plus 4 days per diem at $25 per day	$342	

	Requested	Donated
Local travel		
Exec. Director at 100 mi. per x 12 mos. x 10¢ per mi.	$120	
(2) Community Organizers at 500 mi. per mo. x 12 mos. x 10¢ per mi.	$1,200	

Out-of-town travel is a very vulnerable section of your budget. Plan and justify as completely as you can.

E. Telephones

Remember installation costs! Put in the number of instruments you will need times the expected monthly cost per instrument. Justify any extensive out-of-town calling that you will have to do.

F. Other Costs

This catch-all category can include the following:
1. Postage
2. Fire, theft and liability insurance
3. Dues in professional associations paid by the agency
4. Subscriptions
5. Publications, the cost of which may be broken up into:
   a. printing
   b. typesetting
   c. addressing, if done by a service
   d. mailing (separate and distinct from office postage above)
6. Any other items that don't logically fit elsewhere

A NOTE about Indirect Costs

Some programs, particularly those conducted within a large institution, such as a college or university, also include an indirect cost figure. Indirect costs are paid to the host institution in return for its rendering certain services to the project. The host may manage the bookkeeping and payroll, assume some responsibility for overseeing the project, take care of maintenance and utility costs, etc. The first time an institution conducts a federally funded program it projects what these indirect costs will be. Subsequently there is an audit by the federal government, and an indirect cost figure is fixed which will hold for the institution for all subsequent federal grants until the time of the next audit.

Exercise:
Critiquing a Sample Problem Statement

Trying to absorb some of the material that has been written about proposal preparation is only half the battle. The other half involves applying what you know to real situations. This activity puts you in the seat of the proposal reviewer and requires you to use your wisdom to critique one section of a sample proposal. A checklist for reviewing problem statements is provided as a guide, but participants should keep in mind that "real world" reviewers can be as subjective as anyone else.

The Process:

1. Select a discussion leader, or two, if more than seven or eight people are present.

2. Pass out copies of the article, *Program Planning and Proposal Writing,* and ask everyone to read it (25-30 minutes). The reading can be done prior to the meeting to save time.

3. Devote another 15-30 minutes to a discussion of the article (see the **Discussion Questions** on this page).

4. Separate into groups with a maximum of seven or eight people in each.

5. Hand out copies of the checklist for reviewing the sample problem statement. Allow 5-10 minutes for participants to read it. Ask for comments, additional items, and opinions about the checklist.

6. Distribute the sample problem statement and ask participants to spend 10 minutes reading it.

7. Ask each participant to jot down their comments about the quality, content and suggested improvements, using the checklist as a guide.

8. Solicit each person's overall impression of the problem statement, recording them on newsprint.

9. Dicuss the criticisms and suggested improvements in small groups.

10. Compare the suggestions made by each small group.

QUESTIONS FOR DISCUSSING "PROGRAM PLANNING AND PROPOSAL WRITING"

- *What else do you need to know about writing a proposal?*

- *How do the ideas presented in this article compare with what you know about proposal writing?*

- *How can you apply the information in this article to your present fund-raising efforts?*

- *How have proposals you've written differed from the suggestions in the article?*

Sample Problem Statement

Although $70 billion is poured into American public schools every year, there are an estimated 23 million adult citizens who don't have the minimal reading, writing and calculating skills needed to function in modern society. There is abundant evidence documenting illiteracy as a widespread problem. The 1970 census counted 1.4 million illiterate adults in the **US**. Experts say this figure is much too low because it only indicates completed grade levels. Researchers are now measuring "functional" illiteracy in order to include those who cannot apply reading, writing and math skills to everyday life. Some of the evidence is cited below:

- Navy recruiting stations reject 9 out of 10 applicants because they can't pass the initial screening test.

- The National Assessment of Educational Progress estimates that 13% of the 17 year-olds still in school are illiterate.

- Thirty-three state legislatures have enacted "minimum competency" standards for public schools.

- A government survey showed that 1/3 of U.S. companies with more than 10,000 employees have begun remedial education programs for their workers.

Locally, 50,000 adults over the age of 16 in Ourcity have no high school diploma, and one out of 10 adults over 25 didn't attend school beyond the sixth grade, according to the 1970 **US Census.** School department officials estimate that 20% of the adult population in Ourcity is illiterate. Clearly, this is a problem of tremendous local and national importance.

What does being illiterate mean in our society? It means that people can't fill out job applications, count change at the supermarket, use telephone directories, read road maps or perform a host of other simple tasks that are taken for granted. The National Assessment of Educational Progress gave a group of 17 year-olds a traffic ticket and asked them to find the date of the last day the fine could be paid; over half of them couldn't.

Most illiterate adults also suffer emotionally. Low self-esteem, anger, resentment and feeling "cheated" are common. Worse, people try to hide their handicap, feeling ashamed that they can't perform simple tasks. One job-seeker asked a friend to come to an interview to help him fill out the job application.

Why is illiteracy a problem? Learning disabilities and poor instruction in schools account for many of these cases. School officials readily admit that schools just don't have the time to cope with students whose basic skills are deficient. So the further such a student goes in school, the further he falls behind his classmates. Some experts think that teacher training should include more courses in teaching basic skills so that all teachers are adequately prepared to teach reading.

Experts also think that modern culture plays a role in the illiteracy problem. The primary offender, they say, is television, because it makes people "passive receivers" of messages while not allowing them to reshape their own ideas. The widespread use of electronic media, in general, has replaced reading as a form of leisure activity.

Checklist for Critiquing a Sample Problem Statement

☐ What is the nature of the problem being discussed?

☐ What are the underlying causes of the problem?

☐ How does the organization document the nature and extent of the problem? What kind of data is used?

☐ How significant is this problem compared with others in the community, region or state?

☐ What have other attempts to solve the problem accomplished, not accomplished?

☐ Is the information presented logically and clearly?

☐ Are there words that you don't understand?

☐ Who has recognized this as a serious need (Presidential or gubernatorial commission, experts in the field, legislature, research and planning institutions)?

☐ Overall, does the applicant organization appear to have a good grasp of what the problem is?

☐ Using these questions as a guide, does the sample problem statement give you enough information to understand the problem, too little information, or too much?

"Meaningless statistics were up one-point-five per cent this month over last month."

Reprinted from Dollars and Sense, 324 Somerville Ave., Somerville.

Reviewing and Editing Proposals

"My Lord!
Can that thing be right?"

Drawings by Oldden; Copyright 1968
The New Yorker Magazine, Inc.

Deadlines come up too fast; you keep adding to the proposal, and what happens? There's no time left to review and edit the proposal, so it gets shoved into an envelope and delivered or mailed. But a thorough review of what's been written serves several functions:

- It helps eliminate unnecessary or redundant information.

- It allows a quality check. Is there a logical flow from section to section? Are words defined, typographical errors corrected, etc.?

- It serves as a completeness test. Does the proposal state clearly what the program and organization are trying to accomplish? Are the necessary appendices attached?

- It allows the time for the policy-making board to give its final approval and familiarize itself with the contents of the entire proposal.

There are several ways to review proposals. One is for the fundraiser to do it alone or invite comments from members and staff. Another is to present them to the policy-making board; still another is to involve a group of "outsiders" in the review process.

The next activity focuses on the latter, because although it is used less frequently than the other methods it offers the chance for some feedback that wouldn't come from those within the organization.

Group review can turn up some unexpected information. I once sat in on a review process where each reviewer was asked to summarize the ideas in the proposal. Five very different perceptions of the proposal were expressed, so it was apparent that the proposal was not a clear presentation of the program. Discussion then followed on how to eliminate the confusion in the proposal; each reviewer suggested changes that needed to be made. In another review group, major questions were raised about the budget. Discussion focused on how to change the budget format to be more clear about what was being requested from the funding source.

Exercise:
Group Review of Proposals

The main advantage of inviting comments from an outside group of reviewers is to pinpoint areas that are confusing to people who aren't familiar with the organization. Reviewers need not be "professional"; anyone who's had some fund-raising experience can comment on what makes sense in the proposal and what doesn't. A group of reviewers can be composed of the following:

- fundraisers from other nonprofit organizations;

- people who have received funding from the funding source to whom you're applying;

- people who know nothing about your organization;

- anyone with good writing skills.

Once you've completed a proposal and want some reaction to it prior to sending it to the funding source, select five reviewers. Give each one a copy of your proposal and any guidelines published by the funding source. A checklist for reviewing proposals is included in this activity as an additional guide for reviewers.

The Process:

1. Select a discussion leader.

2. Establish "rules" for giving constructive criticism as needed. Example: Reviewers may be asked to offer positive comments *before* critical ones. Or reviewers may want to "de-personalize" their comments by saying, "What is meant by _____?" rather than, "What do *you* mean by _____?"

3. Ask the proposal-writer to identify specific things (s)he would like feedback on (style, grammar, sequence, format, program design, budget).

4. Pass out the **Checklist for Reviewing Proposals** and allow 10-15 minutes for people to read it. The proposal-writer can emphasize specific questions on the checklist (s)he would like reviewers to concentrate on.

5. Hand out copies of the proposal. Allow enough time for reviewers to read the entire proposal. Another option is to mail both the checklist and the proposal to reviewers *prior* to the meeting.

6. Ask each person to give their overall impression of the proposal (5 minutes per person).

7. Taking each section of the proposal separately, ask for the reviewers' comments, allowing at least 10 minutes per person. You may also want to ask each person to summarize what's been said in each section. The discussion leader should note differences in the summaries and concentrate on those differences.

8. The discussion leader can record "suggestions for improving the proposal" during the discussion. This list can be used to summarize the meeting, and suggestions that all reviewers agree with can be highlighted.

Possible Follow-up:

"Support networks" for fundraisers are becoming increasingly common. One role for such a network is reviewing proposals that members of the network have already written. The review process in this activity can be used each time a member of the network completes a proposal.

Drawing by Brenda Yellock

Checklist for Reviewing Proposals

The questions in this checklist are ones that many reviewers ask as they read through proposals. You may want to use this as a guide to review someone else's proposal or to help you write and edit a proposal of your own. The questions correspond to the format suggested in Program Planning and Proposal Writing *and should be adapted when it's appropriate for different funding sources. This list is by no means comprehensive, since each funding source has its own criteria for evaluating proposals. Space is provided for you to make additions to the list.*

Proposal Summary

☐ What is being requested from the funding source?

☐ Is the applicant organization adequately described (purpose, location, size, qualifications)?

☐ What are the major components of the proposed program?

☐ Does the summary "stand by itself," describing briefly the applicant organization and proposed program?

☐ Does the summary interest you enough to make you want to read more?

☐ Other questions:

Proposal Introduction

☐ Is the history of the organization adequately described (origins, purpose, major successes and accomplishments)?

☐ Who has funded the group in the past?

☐ Do you have a clear picture of the organization?

- What is the size and composition of its membership, volunteers, staff and board of directors?

- What geographic area is the group working in and what are the characteristics of the people the group is working with?

- What is the size of the annual budget?

- What is the structure of the organization?

☐ Does the organization appear to be capable of handling the amount of money being requested?

- How does this amount compare with previous funding?

- What other funding sources have contributed to this particular program?

☐ Has this organization received any support from members, clients and/or the local community?

- Does the organization attempt to conduct some projects that generate some income?

- What kind of in-kind contributions does the group receive and from whom?

- Do leaders in the community appear to support the work of this group?

- What kind of recognition has the organization received (media coverage, endorsements, etc.)?

☐ Is there something "special" about this organization; something that makes it different from other groups?

☐ Can you summarize the primary strengths of the organization?

☐ What are the capabilities of the staff and volunteers?

☐ Are the staff's qualifications sufficient to carry out the program as described or will

57

additional staff be
needed?

☐ Other questions:

☐ Other questions:

have happened as a result
of the project?

☐ Other questions:

Problem or Need Statement

☐ What is the nature of the
problem described in the
proposal?

☐ What are the underlying
causes of the problem?

☐ How does the organization
document the nature and
extent of the problem?
What kind of data is used?

☐ How significant is this
problem compared with
others in that community,
region, or state?

☐ What have other attempts
to solve the problem
accomplished/not
accomplished?

☐ Does this program duplicate similar activities of
other organizations?

☐ Overall, does the
organization appear to
have a good grasp of what
the problem is?

☐ Who has recognized this
as a serious need (Presi-
dential or gubernatorial
commission, experts in
the field, legislatures,
research and planning
institutions)?

☐ Are there words or terms
that need definition?

Objectives

☐ Do the objectives relate
to the problem statement
described in the previous
section?

☐ How specific and
measurable are the
objectives?

☐ Do the objectives say
what the **organization** hopes
to accomplish (e.g. "Our
objective is to train maroon
elephants to count from one
to 10.") or do they show
how this program will affect
program participants (e.g.
"Eighty percent of the
maroon elephants in Our-
city will be able to count
from one to 10 upon
command.")?

☐ Do the objectives sound
realistic or does it sound
like mountains will have to
be moved?

☐ Are the objectives ex-
pressed in terms of
outcomes, naming
specific things that will

Method Or Activities

☐ Do the activities relate to
the problem statement and
objectives?

☐ Is there a timetable or work
plan that explains the scope
and sequence of the
activities?

☐ Is there any "fuzziness;"
does the project seem to
be developed sufficiently?

☐ Does the applicant explain
why this approach was
chosen over other pos-
sible approaches?

☐ How does the applicant
propose to coordinate its
activities with other
agencies?

☐ Has the organization had
experience running this kind
of program? If not, what
specific resources or skills
will be needed to run an
effective program? Does the
organization have access to
these skills or resources?

☐ How does this program
relate to others that the
organization is running?
(Is it top priority, second,
third, etc.?)

☐ How were the ideas and
details for this project
developed? By whom?

58

☐ Other questions:

☐ Other questions:

☐ What are the projected sources of income for the project?

☐ Other questions:

Evaluation

☐ How will the organization know when it has succeeded, failed or done a mediocre job?

☐ What specific "milestones" will help measure the progress of the program?

☐ Who is responsible for doing the evaluation? How much will it cost?

☐ How will the data collected for the evaluation be used?
  • What specific decisions will the evaluation results help make?

☐ What will be evaluated and how?

☐ Who will see the final results of the evaluation?

Future Funding

☐ What are the organization's plans for obtaining funding next year? the year after? in five years?

☐ What percentage of future budgets will be derived from members, participants, fees or community support?

☐ Other questions:

Budget

☐ Is there a budget for the proposed programs *and* one for the entire organization?

☐ Does the format of the budget make sense?

☐ Are the costs too high or low?

☐ Are there too many or too few staff positions for the proposed program?

☐ How do the costs of this program compare with those of similar programs?

☐ Are *all* the costs for the program included in the budget?

☐ Are there cost items that don't appear to be necessary to run the program?

Questions That Don't Usually Get Asked But Should Be

☐ Will this program increase or decrease participants' dependency on this and other organizations? How?

☐ What assumptions about people does the design of this program make (e.g. does it assume that people don't work because they're lazy, unskilled, or there aren't enough jobs)?

Discussion Questions:

• *What have you learned about proposal writing from these activities? from your own experiences?*

• *How can you share your perspective on proposal writing with others in your group?*

• *What kind of information, help, and support does a proposal-writer need from members of the organization?*

• *What are some things you can do to make sure there will be sufficient time to review a proposal before it has to be submitted?*

Step 10:
Proposal Follow-up

"Am I to assume that you are not in complete accord with my counter offer?"

Having breathed a sigh of relief and now thinking that the worst is over, it's tempting for fundraisers to send off a proposal, and wait. And wait. And wait.

This is called the passive approach. While it's reasonable to expect funding sources to acknowledge receiving proposals and to notify applicants of funding decisions, this doesn't always happen.

A quick phone call to the funding source a few weeks after submitting the proposal can relieve much of the waiting-in-the-dark frustration. A fear of being "pushy" prevents some fundraisers from doing this, but as long as you're not bugging the funding source every day, follow-up is advisable. Possible questions for the call are:

"Have you had a chance to read our proposal?"

"Do you have any questions about the proposal or budget?"

"When will you be able to talk with me about the proposal?"

"When do you expect to have made your final decision?"

"Are there specific points in the proposal that need clarification?"

"Do you need additional materials (last year's financial statement, for example)?"

Another aspect of the follow-up is negotiation, or at least the willingness to negotiate. This is why the fundraiser needs to have a clear notion of what compromises will be acceptable to the staff, board and members of the organization prior to the follow-up contact.

If, during the follow-up, it becomes apparent that the funding source is interested in the program but has reservations, push for clarification of the points in question. Any program changes that have been discussed on the telephone should always be summarized in a follow-up letter to the funding source. Before making any commitments to program changes, consider the questions below.

• What changes are the funding source suggesting?

• What is the nature of the changes? How will they affect the proposed program?

• Have the group's staff/board/members had the opportunity to express their opinions about the proposed changes?

• What are the advantages and disadvantages of the changes?

• Are the changes acceptable to the group as a whole?

Step 11:
Interview with a Funding Source

Because most citizen groups operate on shoestring budgets and occupy less than glamorous offices, a fundraiser's first visit to the funding source may be a shock. Sitting in a gaily upholstered chair and peeking through a jungle of tropical plants, it's no wonder that novice fundraisers are somewhat intimidated. And there's usually an imposing desk or table to separate grantee from grantor.

This is the stereotypical image, of course, but you'll certainly experience a similar scene at least once. Whatever the actual physical surroundings, fundraisers need to be able to adapt to any situation. Aside from being interviewed in an environment that's foreign to most citizen groups, there are a number of other issues:

How Many People Should Go to the Interview?

Often, the fundraiser meets the funding source alone because it simplifies the negotiation process and a one-to-one conversation is easier to follow. Another option is to take two people to an interview, either the executive director or a member of the organization's board of directors. One or two people are sufficient; a third person is about the upper limit. Although it would be nice to pack the stands with a cheering squad, you risk turning the meeting into a circus with more than three people.

If more than one person goes to the interview, someone should be designated the primary spokesperson, with the other(s) providing supplemental information or their personal perspectives. Some citizen groups go so far as to develop hand signals for use during the interview—adjusting a watch band to indicate that someone is talking too much, etc. Better yet, the ability to "read" the nonverbal expressions of your colleagues will give you an edge during the interview.

Who Should Meet With the Funding Source?

Here are some questions to help you decide who should go to the interview:

- *Does the person meet people easily?*

- *Is the person able to articulate clearly the goals and needs of the organization?*

- *Is the person knowledgeable enough to respond to specific questions about the program?*

- *Why do you think this particular person should be in on the interview?*

- *Does the person have an easy-going manner and feel comfortable in various situations?*

What Kind of Questions Will the Funding Source Ask?

Think about the contributions you've made or membership dues you've paid to various organizations over the years. What questions about that group ran through your mind before you wrote out a check? Many of these same questions (assuming you had some) could pop up during an interview with a funding source. One strategy is to *anticipate* what the questions will be by brainstorming with a group of people a list of all the possible questions that could be asked. A second strategy is to ask another person to play the part of a grantor and have a practice session. Another option is to try the activity on the next page—a role-play involving a groups of people in a "mock" interview situation.

62

Role-Play:
Interview with a Funding Source

The purpose of this activity is to give citizen group members some practice in being interviewed by a funding source. Discussion following the role-play is an integral part of the activity, enabling participants to analyze and summarize what they learned from it. People need not have previous fund-raising experience to take part in this activity. Common sense and imagination are the only skills needed.

The Process:

1. Select a discussion leader to explain and coordinate the role-play.

2. Divide into three groups of two to five people each.
    The three groups are:
    Group A: Community Action Services for Employment (CASE)
    Group B: Support Training and Rehabilitation (STAR)
    Group C: Trustees of the Dusty Dollar Foundation

3. The discussion leader should read the following background information to the whole group before starting:

    CASE and STAR have submitted proposals to the Dusty Dollar Foundation. The foundation has invited each group to an interview with the trustees. The foundation has informed both groups that these interviews do not imply a funding commitment, although the proposals from each group are very impressive.

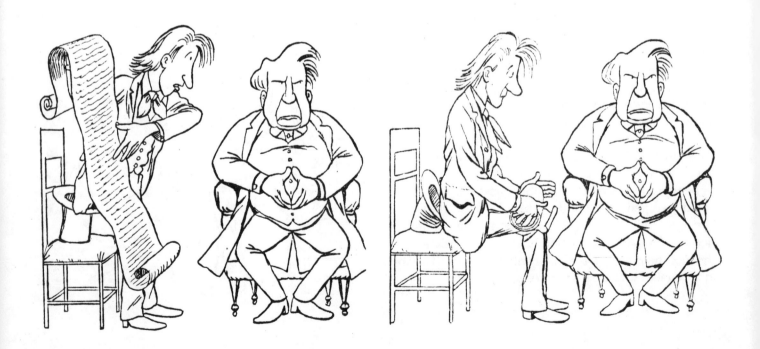

4. The sequence for the role-play is:

I (10 min.)
Divide into three groups; read role-play; ask questions.

II (25 min.)
Each group develops a strategy for the interview.

III (25 min.)
Group A meets with foundation, while Group B observes.

IV (25 min.)
Group B meets with foundation, while Group A observes.

V (10 min.)
Foundation decides how to allocate its money.

VI (30 min.)
Discussion: What happened during the role-play?

5. Pass out the role-play materials. Groups A and B do *not* get copies of each other's proposal outlines. NOTE: Sketchy details are included for each proposal. Groups A and B are asked to invent program details as needed.

6. Go through the role-play. The discussion leader should keep track of time and make sure that everyone understands what they are supposed to be doing.

7. Discuss what happened during the role-play (see suggested questions for discussion at the end of the role-play).

64

Note: Distribute to Groups A and C only.

Community Action Services for Employment (CASE)

Purpose of Group: Designs and implements programs for opening the job market to those presently unemployable.

Present program: **Family Employment Planning Project (FEPP):** A program which allows families to replace "heads of households" with a multi-earner income process (helping adults and teenagers to become wage earners). Program involves counseling, using skilled staff and paraprofessional staff to work with individual families. Present budget is $100,000 annually with funds provided by:

- U.S. Dept. of Labor - $45,000

- U.S. Dept. of Commerce - $25,000

- Mass. Dept. of Labor - $15,000

- Ford Foundation - $15,000

Proposal: Current proposal is for a program which would re-train individuals laid off due to industrial changes and help those entering the job market for the first time. Also, family-training workshops, consisting of multi-family sessions that develop group awareness and peer support structure for families, making the transition from "head-of-household" to "family-earning process," are proposed. A community newsletter will be distributed to supplement the training sessions. Training consists of helping families and individuals understand the situation and problem, know the alternatives, and develop resources and skills for solutions. Plans also call for working closely with local companies in developing necessary resources, skills and training. CASE has requested a minimum of $30,000 from the Dusty Dollar Foundation.

Group B: Proposal Outline and Program   Note: Distribute to Groups B and C only.

Support Training and Rehabilitation (STAR)

Purpose of Group: STAR provides technical assistance for those who have been unemployed for two or more years due to criminal record, illness, or handicaps.

Present Program: STAR is helping those re-entering the workforce after long-term unemployment, using six on-site (company) counselling centers. The program involves monitoring and evaluating newly employed people at these six participating companies to determine individual problems and needs, skills and resources, and the appropriate type of counselling necessary. The process provides support-base through individual and group counselling, thereby easing the transition and assuring employment success.

The annual budget is $100,000. Revenue for staff and counsellors come from federal and state sources; monitoring and evaluation materials and staff funding come from private foundations and most overhead and materials come from participating companies.

Proposal: STAR proposes to expand the present program to include those unemployed two or more years who have not yet located job prospects. Counselling and training would be developed to design and locate possible careers and employment opportunities. More companies would be enlisted as participants and staff specialists would be hired to:

- train in specific employable skills;
- establish on-the-job training;
- assist people to learn and expand their personal skills.

Correspondingly, STAR proposes to train businesses to develop employment opportunities and on-the-job training. These clients would learn to anticipate and prevent problems, involve workers in planning, develop job satisfaction procedures, create successful and long-term employment situations, and offer basic counselling services to employees. First year costs are projected to be at least $100,000 for expansion. STAR has requested a minimum of $30,000 from the Dusty Dollar Foundation.

Group C   Note: Distribute to Group C only

Dusty Dollar Foundation Trustees

You are the trustees of the Dusty Dollar Foundation, a corporate foundation in Massachusetts that distributes $200,000/year in grants (see the attached blurb from your annual report for a description of funding priorities, etc.). Your last meeting of the year is coming up and only $20,000 remains for grant allocations. Out of the 30 proposals received for this meeting, two were selected for final consideration. Both proposals are for job training in neighboring towns. Each group has requested a minimum of $30,000.

Some role possibilities for the trustees are suggested below but there are many more, so be creative. You could be a person who:

- hasn't read the proposals and asks irrelevant questions;

- questions how realistic the budget is;

- suggests changes in the program design;

- wants to talk about the philosophy of training "disadvantaged" people and family earning units;

- questions the long-term impact of the program;

- wants to know how the program will be continued in the future, beyond the first year;

- wants to get the interviews over with and interrupts the interview;

- thinks that family earning units are unrealistic and that the primary earning responsibility is a male role;

- has stereotyped images of handicapped and criminal offenders; sees them as needing extra attention and as security risks;

- likes the programs and tries to convince other trustees of their feasibility.

TASK:

1. You have invited the two groups to an interview. **Decide what questions to ask them** during the interview. (25 min.)

2. The two applicant groups will then meet with you. (25 min. for each group)

3. Decide how you will allocate the $20,000. (10 min.)

DUSTY DOLLAR FOUNDATION, INC.
1978 Annual Report
Year End: May 31, 1978

DESCRIPTION OF CONTRIBUTION PROGRAM

Dusty Dollar Foundation, Inc. was set up in 1951 to handle charitable contribution activities of the Dusty Dollar Corporation and its plants across the United States. Since 1951, $4,177,000 has been distributed to charitable organizations in communities where Dusty Dollar plants are located.

Priorities for this past year were (1) urban and community-based programs, particulary community health centers, manpower development, community education and criminal justice programs; (2) higher education; (3) hospital building funds; and (4) United Way campaigns. Projects that show a substantial amount of community support, cooperation with other organizations, and a history of effective programming will be given careful attention.

Applicants are requested to submit written proposals, detailing the organization's history, present programs, plans for the future and a budget for the proposed program. The foundation does not supply application forms to applicants.

Discussion Questions for the Role-Play:

When the role-play is finished, the discussion leader should summarize what happened and ask for general impressions. That can be used as the basis for answering the questions below.

- *Which questions asked by the funding source were the most difficult to answer? Why?*

- *What kind of pre-interview preparation would have made the presentations better?*

- *What was the overall tone of each interview?*

- *Which interview went best? Why?*

- *What other questions do you think the funding source could or should have asked?*

- *Did you find yourself stretching the truth to please the funding source?*

- *Were there questions that the applicants should have asked the funding source?*

- *What are the differences between this role-play and an interview situation you might find yourself in?*

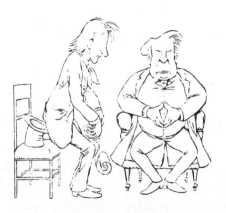

Funding Source Site Visit

(A project director preparing for a site visit.)

Reprinted from Workforce

A site visit is when the funding source comes knocking on your door to see how the organization operates, meet the staff, and see the facilities. Usually funding sources don't do this until a fairly advanced stage in the decision-making process. Government agencies and some large foundations are the primary users of site visits as a tool for evaluating grant applications.

Planning the site visit could include the following questions:

- *What do you want to get across during the visit?*

- *How can that be communicated most effectively?*

- *Who should talk with the visitor(s)? For how long?*

- *What's the schedule for the site visit?*

You might also want to talk with other organizations that have received money from the funding source and ask them what to expect. Once again, the key to preparing for a site visit is anticipating what the funding source will want to see and what questions they will have.

Discussion Questions:

- *If you have ever been interviewed or visited by a funding source and you could re-live that experience, what would you have done differently?*

- *If you've never been interviewed or visited by a funding source, what do you imagine it would be like?*

- *Do you know any other organizations that have been visited by funding sources? Can you question them?*

- *What needs to be done in preparation for an interview or a site visit?*

- *How will you follow-up your meeting with the funding source?*

Step 12: Decision of the Funding Source

It could take months, sometimes a year to get to this point — don't hold your breath. When the official-looking letter or package arrives, hold it up to the light and rip it open. Depending on the contents, some possible responses are:

"We are pleased to inform you . . ."

- Scream with delight and head for the bank.

- Head for the bank and write a thank-you letter.

- Notify the staff, members and board of directors, and head for the bank.

- If you still need additional funding for the program, ask the funding source if they would be willing to introduce you to other funding sources on your list.

- Make sure you understand any stipulations or "conditions" attached to the grant and put them in writing.

- Ask the funding source if you can publish a press release in the local newspaper about the grant.

- Review with the funding source the procedures for submitting "progress reports."

- If your funding source will not release the funds until matching funds are raised from other sources, notify the funding source as soon as matching funds are raised.

"We are sorry to inform you . . ."

- Write a letter thanking them for their time.

- Put them on your mailing list, so they won't forget who you are.

- Call and ask if they could spend 10 minutes explaining why the request was turned down.

- Chalk it up to experience and think about what you learned this time around.

- Ask if the funding source would be willing to introduce you to other funding sources on your list or call them on your behalf.

- Some federal agencies hold de-briefing sessions. Reviewers' comments are read and the review process is explained. Ask if the funding source holds such sessions.

Discussion Questions:

- *Did the funding source give you any indication of why the project wasn't funded?*

- *Why do you think the project wasn't funded?*

- *If funding was approved, do you know what the reporting requirements will be?*

- *What have you learned from this experience that you could share with others in the group?*

Grassroots Fund-Raising

This is grassroots fund-raising in its simplest form. But it works. Whether it's benefits, door-to-door canvassing or membership dues, raising money in the community is the backbone of most citizen groups' budgets.

The **advantages** of this kind of fund-raising are:

- It's an indication of member commitment and community support.

- Everyone can help; special "expertise" is not required.

- It's creative—the realm of possibilities is infinite.

- It enables members to increase their own skills.

- It builds good teamwork.

- It brings in money with "no strings attached."

- It removes dependency on traditional funding sources.

In order for all that to happen, careful planning, time and hard work are necessary. The activities in this section will get you started but you're encouraged to read the **Grass Roots Fundraising Book** by Joan Flanagan, for ideas and detailed information about specific events. It includes everything from "How to Rebound From a Fundloser" to the intricacies of ad books and movie premiers.

Membership Dues

Asking for support (financial and otherwise) from members is one of the best evaluation tools around. It's a good indication of member commitment to the organization and can tell you whether past and planned activities are perceived as relevant to members' needs and interests. Accountability is an important aspect of financial support. When groups seek grants from the government, corporations, churches and foundations, they are accountable to these grantors. Setting up a dues structure shifts the accountability from grantors to members.

This activity is divided into four parts, each dealing with an aspect of dues structures: (1) preliminary questions, (2) establishing membership dues, (3) options for dues structures, and (4) benefits for dues-paying members. The best setting for this activity is an informal meeting involving as many of the group's "members" as possible. Select a discussion leader who is adept at summarizing and keeping discussions focused.

Part I: Preliminary Questions

"Membership" has taken the form of paying money to an organization in return for receiving a monthly newsletter or packet of materials. There are, however, other definitions of membership. To eliminate any confusion, it is essential to devote some time to defining terms. Allow enough time on each question for the group to come to agreement.

- *Who are the present members of the group?*

- *Who are the potential members of the group?*

- *Presently, how does someone become a member?*

- *What is the role of members in the group?*

  - *workers (staff and volunteers)*

  - *people who receive services*

  - *people who give money because they agree with the principles of the group*

  - *decision-makers of the group*

  - *other:*

- *What should the role of members be?*

- *How will setting up a dues structure affect the organization?*

- *Will a dues structure change the relationship between members and the organization? If so, how?*

- *What are the advantages and disadvantages of establishing a dues structure?*

- *What role should membership dues play in the finances of the organization?*

  - *a source of matching funds for grants*

  - *pay most or all of the costs needed to keep the group operating at a minimal level*

  - *support specific activities, such as a newsletter*

  - *cover all operating expenses*

Part II: Establishing Membership Dues

A decision about the importance of dues is critical in determining what the membership fee will be. Some groups regard dues as the "backbone" of the organization.
These groups establish membership fees based on minimal operating needs (assuming
the budget will be supplemented by income from fund-raising events and/or grants).
Other groups see dues as "gravy" — a way of bringing in additional support. In the
latter case, expenses are projected for the year and sources of income are identified
(grants and fund-raising events). The gap between projected income and expenses
then determines the amount to be raised from dues.

*Review the decisions made in Part I of this activity, focusing on the last question.
One way to clarify issues and help the group to come to consensus is to list the
advantages and disadvantages of each option.*

*Once the group has decided on the role of dues, make a list of all the projected
expenses that membership dues will cover. Then make a realistic estimate of the
number of dues-paying members that can be recruited by the end of the year.*

Projected Expenses to Be Covered by Membership Dues

1. Example: newsletter $500
2.
3.
4.
5.
6.
7.
8.
9.
10.

A. TOTAL EXPENSES TO BE
PAID FOR BY MEMBERSHIP
DUES   _____

B. ESTIMATED NUMBER OF
DUES-PAYING MEMBERS
BY THE END OF THE YEAR   # _____

    MEMBERSHIP FEE/PERSON $
     (A ÷ B)

---

*This dollar amount might seem to be too high for some members to pay. Can
the number of members to be recruited be increased? Can some of the options
in Part III make the dues structure more equitable?*

Part III: Options for Dues Structures

There are a number of possibilities for making a dues structure as equitable as possible.

Spend 10 minutes reading these options and adding others. Decide which options are more appropriate for your group, given the compostion of your membership.

Flat fee: This is the simplest method; it's based on anticipated expenses divided by the projected number of dues-paying members.

Sweat equity: So that dues don't exclude people who can't afford to pay, you might want to offer some kind of exchange. It could be volunteering a certain number of hours per month or an in-kind contribution, such as chairs and tables for the office.

Discounts: A special reduction in dues can be offered to specific population groups, such as the elderly or students.

Sliding scale: Some groups set up a dues scale based on the ability to pay, usually using income ranges.

Example: Annual Income	Dues
$5,000 or under	$5
$5,000 - 8,000	$8
$8,000 - 10,000	$10

Categories of membership: Groups can maintain a one-person one-vote principle and establish categories of membership.

Example:	
Patron	$100 or more
Friend	$50 - $100
Supporter	$25 - $50
Family membership	$25
Individual membership	$15

It's not necessary to provide different benefits for each membership category, although some groups choose to publicly recognize major supporters (both volunteers and donors).

Other options:

Once the group has chosen one or a combination of options, review the expenses listed in **Part II** and estimate the number and type of supporters needed to meet the expenses.

Example:	Total expenses to be raised from membership dues	$_____
	Number of members to be recruited	**Revenue from membership dues**
	No. individuals at $15/person: _____	$_____
	No. families at $25: _____	$_____
	No. elderly memberships at $5/person: _____	$_____

This will undoubtedly take considerable work but the result should be an accurate assessment of the number of members you need to recruit and the amount they will pay.

Reprinted from No Bosses Here by Vocations for Social Change, Cambridge, Mass.

Part IV: Benefits for Dues-Paying Members

Will members receive any specific benefits for paying annual dues? This does give people an incentive for paying their dues but it also costs money. Groups need to decide what, if any, membership benefits there will be and the costs of providing those benefits.

Brainstorm a list of possible benefits, using the list below to begin the brainstorm.

Item	Cost per member to provide each item
Bumperstickers	$_____
Pins	$_____
Membership cards	$_____
Decals	$_____
Newsletter	$_____
Member-only events (dinners, dances, etc.)	$_____
Vote/decision-making	$_____ (none) _____
Other:	$_____
	$_____
	$_____
	$_____
	$_____
TOTAL COSTS PER MEMBER	$_____
ANTICIPATED REVENUE FROM MEMBERSHIP DUES	$_____
COST OF MEMBER BENEFITS	$_____
NET INCOME FROM DUES	$_____

Suggested follow-up:

Once a dues structure is established, the group may want to set up a membership committee to coordinate the recruitment of members and monitor the membership drive. For example, suppose six months have passed and the number of family memberships is lower than the original estimate. The membership committee might want to make a special effort to recruit families. Some organizations establish monthly quotas for membership drives and use the quotas to monitor their progress.

Fund-Raising Events

Bake sales, raffles, tag sales. Is there a citizen group left who hasn't had one? Unfortunately, some citizen groups have become discouraged with the amount of time and work it takes to hold fund-raising events. "We're tired of doing bake sales; we want to write a grant and get all that money in one bundle instead of in dribs and drabs." At first glance, grant-writing does seem to be a viable substitute, but here's the reality.

Events	Grants
• Time-consuming	• Also time-consuming; funding sources have to be identified, proposals written, and the funding decision can take from three months to a year
• Brings in new members	• Grant-writing never results in new members members
• Fun	• Few fundraisers think of the grant process as being fun
• May or may not bring in enough money; on the other hand, money raised can be used for any type of activity	• Usually have "strings attached." Funding for specific projects is more common than unrestricted grants

If members seem reluctant to plan another event, try some of these ideas:

• Ask for everyone's ideas about possible events. They're likely to think of activities that would be fun for them.

• Ask everyone to read the **Grass Roots Fundraising Book**, by Joan Flanagan, for inspiration and ideas.

• Ask members who enjoy planning events to invite two or three other people to a meeting to discuss possible events. Enthusiasm is catching.

• Give incentives to workers—a free dinner, free raffle tickets, all the wine they can drink, etc.

Once over that hurdle, the next task is to begin planning. The major steps are (1) making a list of all the possible events you could do, (2) choosing one or more of the ideas, (3) itemizing costs of putting on the event, (4) setting an income goal, (5) preparing for the event, and (6) post-event discussion.

The next activity outlines some of the aspects of these steps.

Drawing by Brenda Yellock

"What?! You mean the charity ball was last week?"

Exercise:

Choosing an Event

The Process:

1. Select a discussion leader and tape newsprint to the wall.

2. Ask members to brainstorm possible events. The object is to get as many ideas as possible, without critiquing suggestions as they are called out. (10-20 minutes (10-20 minutes)

3. Write the following selection criteria on newsprint, using those that are appropriate and adding your own as needed.

Involving all members in the early planning stages is a good way to recruit workers. Members will probably suggest events in which they would enjoy participating. Once the events are scheduled, work can be delegated to committees.

  • *Will the event be fun?*

  • *How much income will the event generate (estimate)?*

  • *What are the estimated costs of the event?*

  • *Approximately how much "front money" (costs of supplies, film rental, etc.) will be required? How much can the organization afford?*

  • *Will the event bring in new members and give the group some publicity?*

  • *Is the expected income worth the work that will be required?*

4. Discuss each option and select two or three possibilities, using the criteria (20-30 minutes).

Exercise:

How Much will the Event Cost?

The Process:

1. Transfer this chart to newsprint.

Either using past experience with similar events or by calling vendors, the group should begin the event-planning process with cost estimates. If another organization in the community has held a similar event, you might want to contact them to check on the costs.

Cost Item	Estimated Cost	Possible Vendors	Items to be Donated
Printing: tickets posters			
Space: rent			
Paper supplies			
Postage			
Prizes			
Insurance			
Entertainment			
Food			
Other:			

2. Make a list of all items which will involve some expense.

3. Beside each item, estimate expenses. Call vendors if possible to confirm estimates (15 + minutes).

4. Ask members if any of the items can be donated. Does anyone know of space that could be used rent-free? (10 min.)

5. Total all costs.

Exercise:
Projecting Income and Setting Ticket Prices

The Process:

1. Decide how much income the group would like or needs to make from the event. event. Add to that amount the total costs of holding the event. (10 minutes)

Costs:	$200
Desired income:	800
Total income needed:	$1,000

2. Check any records you might have from similar events or check with other groups to see if the income projection is realistic.

Most groups are conscientious about anticipating expenses, but few bother to set an income goal. The advantage of setting an income goal is that workers have an incentive to sell tickets and income will be more likely to meet costs.

3. Estimate the number of tickets that can be sold and divide that into total income needed (5 minutes).

Gross income:	$1,000
No. tickets:	100
Price/ticket:	$10

4. Make several estimates of ticket sales until the price per ticket seems reasonable for members to pay (10 minutes).

Gross income:	$1,000		Gross income:	$1,000
No. tickets:	200		No. tickets:	125
Price/ticket:	$5		Price/ticket:	$8

5. If you plan to have different prices for different groups, project the number of tickets to be sold for each category (10 minutes).

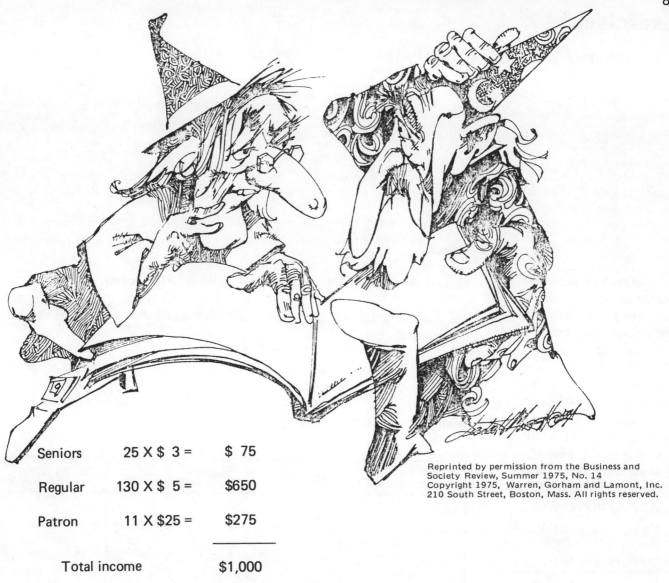

Seniors	25 X $ 3 =	$ 75
Regular	130 X $ 5 =	$650
Patron	11 X $25 =	$275
		————
Total income		$1,000

6. You now know how many tickets will have to be sold. Decide how many tickets one worker can reasonably sell (10 minutes).

Type of Ticket	No. Workers	No. Tickets/ Worker	Price/ Ticket
Seniors	5	5	$ 3
Regular	10	13	$ 5
Patron	2	5.5	$25

7. The end result is an income goal for the event and a plan for achieving it.

Exercise:
Preparing for the Event

The Process:

Careful coordination and plenty of workers with specific tasks and deadlines are the primary concerns in getting ready for an event. Coordination of the event may be handled by a fundraising committee; each committee member would assume responsibility for one aspect of the event. For example, one person could be responsible for coordinating ticket sales; another person, advertising; another, finding performers, speakers and so on.

1. Make a list of all the jobs that need to be done (20 minutes).

2. Ask for a volunteer to take responsibility for seeing that each task is completed (15 minutes).

3. For jobs that require more than one person, find a volunteer coordinator and as many workers as needed.

4. Assign deadline dates for each task (20 minutes).

Task	Deadline	Person Responsible	People Who Are Helping

Possible Follow-up: *Monitor the pre-event activities. You could have weekly meetings and review the Task Chart, asking each member if (s)he's met her/his deadlines. Ticket sales should be reviewed frequently to make sure quotas are being met.*

5. Plan for "disasters." Something will surely go wrong, so anticipate *all* the possible disruptions of the event (rain, not enough food, performers not showing up, etc.). This is best done as a group brainstorm (10 minutes).

6. Next to each disaster, brainstorm measures that could be taken as prevention (15 minutes).

7. Add "disaster contingency plans" to the task list; for example, "get indoor space in case of rain" (10 minutes).

83

Exercise:
What Should we do After the Event?

The Process:

1. Discuss members' reactions to the event, making special note of areas that needed improvement. You could ask workers to write a few paragraphs about changes they would recommend if the event were to be repeated in the future (30 minutes).

2. You might want to start an "Events Notebook," which would contain the following information:

Once the event is over, there's the inevitable clean-up job, returning borrowed items and thank-you letters.

Type of event: Barbecue

Place: Smith's cow pasture

Date held: June 5, 1978

No. attending: 100   Ticket price/person: $4

T-shirts sold: 20 @ $3

Total income: $460   Total costs: $75

Net income: $385   Projected net income: $400

No. workers: 20

Comments: The black flies were unbearable and no one remembered to bring the volleyball. The food was great (salad, corn, soyburgers, iced tea/coffee/milk, strawberry shortcake). Members contributed all but soyburgers, drinks and dessert.

3. Discuss other post-event activities such as thank-yous to workers, final report on income, and future fund-raising events (15 minutes).

Canvassing

Canvassing is knocking on doors and asking for contributions. A well-conceived canvassing plan enables the citizen group to (1) solicit contributions, (2) talk with people face-to-face about the group and the issues, (3) get people's positive and negative reactions to the group's activities, and (4) suggest ways in which interested people can become more involved with the organization. Canvassing also requires a good deal of planning, coordination and lots of canvassers.

The first type of canvassing is the full-time, year-round operation where canvassers are assigned to specific neighborhoods and required to meet a quota, say $60 per night. Canvassers can be paid a flat salary, salary plus commission, or straight commission. Their work is coordinated by field staff coordinators and a canvassing director. Neighborhoods are carefully researched prior to the canvassing. Neighborhoods with dense populations and average annual incomes of $8,000 to $10,000 or more receive the most attention.

The second type of canvassing covers a shorter period of time — a week to three months — and usually coincides with a specific organizing issue. Canvassers often volunteer their time and regard canvassing as a way to raise funds and mobilize support around an issue at the same time.

Whichever type of canvassing is undertaken, the ingredients of a canvassing operation are:

- talking with other groups who are already running a canvassing operation;

- finding out what state and local laws apply to canvassing;

- identifying the geographic area that will be concentrated on;

- setting goals of how much money is to be raised and deadlines for reaching the income goals;

- establishing a structure for coordinating the canvassing;

- preparing written materials — petitions, pamphlets, receipt books;

- recruiting canvassers and dividing up the canvassing area;

- training canvassers — written training materials, "buddy system" canvassing, role-plays;

- monitoring the canvassing — daily bookkeeping, weekly meetings;

- evaluating the canvassing when completed. (Were income goals met? What should have been done differently? Which techniques worked well? Why?)

Training canvassers is one of the critical elements of a successful canvassing operation. Most groups use a combination of training techniques; Massachusetts Fair Share uses these below.

- **Training sessions:** Discussions devoted specifically to canvassing techniques and common situations are helpful introductions. You might want to focus on the kinds of reactions people usually have and ask the canvassers to think up responses to each situation. Canvassing techniques can be learned through role-plays, "problem scenarios" (the trainer sets up a situation and asks canvassers how they would deal with it), and small group discussions.

- **Written materials:** Some groups prepare packets of information for new canvassers. You might want to include recent newspaper articles on the organization, basic facts about the organization or an annual report, and any educational materials that have been prepared by the group. The purpose of these materials is to acquaint the canvasser with past and planned activities.

- **Observation:** Many groups require that potential canvassers spend a few hours observing an experienced canvasser. Then the new canvasser tries knocking on doors, accompanied by an experienced canvasser who observes and provides back-up support when needed.

- **On-going training:** After a week or so of canvassing, new canvassers can be paired up with more experienced canvassers (or someone they've never worked with before). This enables canvassers to share ideas and learn new styles. Regular meetings to discuss problems, questions and difficult situations could also be held.

Canvassing is a foolproof method of raising money but requires careful planning. The best resource for establishing a canvassing operation is other experienced canvassers. They can help evaluate your canvassing plans and suggest effective techniques.

Getting the Most Through the Post: Direct Mail

Everyone from Save the Maple Tree Association to Help the Homeless Elephants Fund does it. The letters that fill your mailbox asking for money are direct mail appeals. Used widely by national nonprofit organizations and some state-wide groups, direct mail is an expensive proposition for smaller citizen groups.

Using this approach, mass mailings are sent to "prospects" — people who have never contributed to the organization. The return on these "prospect mailings" is low—between one and three percent. Once a "prospect" returns a donation, (s)he is placed on the "house list." Mailings to "house lists," which include those who have made contributions in the past, bring in a higher return — between 10 - 20 percent. A direct mail appeal is not a one-time only event. The goal

is to develop a list of contributors and concentrate on those people for subsequent mailings.

For most small- and medium-sized citizen groups, direct mail is an expensive way to attract contributors. If, for example, a group would like to add 1,000 contributors to its "house list," the initial mailing would have to be sent to approximately 100,000 people. Locally-based groups will probably have a difficult time compiling such a large "prospect list," let alone affording the postage.

However, there are some variations on the direct mail theme. One public television station that was producing a program on a rare bird species, for example, sent an appeal to members of bird-watchers' clubs. The mailing focused on a specific event and was sent to a limited group whose interest obviously matched the program. This strategy seems to work well if the prospect list is carefully selected and if the organization is well-established.

Another approach is to prepare an appeal for those who are on the organization's mailing list. Groups that publish newsletters or sell publications have used this technique often, since people on the mailing list (1) already know about the organization and (2) have purchased materials by mail. Small citizen groups will probably find this approach to be the most cost effective. But, like other direct mail appeals, this requires careful maintenance of mailing lists.

Direct mail is an involved process, so readers are encouraged to consult the Resource section for more in-depth analyses of how to prepare a direct mail appeal.

Case Study of Women's Campaign Fund

The Women's Campaign Fund appeal is used here as an example of a good direct mail approach because it's different and successful. Using a stapled booklet (8½" X 11") format, the appeal is immediately distinguished from the standard two-page letter.

The front page of the appeal boasts a "Dear Friend" letter from Sharon Percy Rockefeller, the daughter of Illinois Senator Charles Percy and wife of John D. IV (Jay). It seems incongruous that anyone with the name Rockefeller would be bold enough to ask for money, and that is the major flaw of the booklet.

But the letter itself begins with the statement,"Men run America." First sentences are intended to (1) catch your attention, and (2) elicit a response (hopefully, to read on). This one-liner accomplishes both, assuming a specific readership. The letter continues with succinctly stated facts and ends with a reminder that the Women's Campaign Fund has and is trying to change things. The rest of the booklet follows this style, using carefully selected statistics to make a strong case. The last sentence in the letter suggests a contribution of $25, and this is the only mention in the booklet of a specific dollar request. However, on nearly every page of the booklet, the last sentence reminds the reader that support is needed, echoing the letter.

In general, the approach is good. The Fund presents facts, with small charts and graphs, and avoids the "we-you" question almost entirely. One of the cardinal rules of direct mail appeal letters is that the number of "you's" should outnumber the "we's." Many letters succomb to the "we-we" disease, bombarding the reader with all the marvelous things that "we" had done. By opting for a factual presentation and the use of the third person to describe the Fund's activities, the booklet adopts a more "objective" tone than the usual appeals which use the first person.

A spokesperson for the Fund says that reactions to the booklet have been favorable. Contributors have made positive remarks about the graphics, the chart of political action committee contributions, and the na names of national supporters. Of the 150,000 booklets that have been mailed out, the return is over one percent, fairly good for a relatively new organization. Names of contributors are placed on "house lists" to receive follow-up appeal letters. This is the standard direct mail process — sending out a mass mailing to a specific audience, and doing follow-up mailings to those who contributed the first time around.

The booklet is reproduced on the following pages; these discussion questions may serve as an aid for designing your own direct mail appeal.

- *What's your overall reaction to the booklet?*

- *For whom was the booklet written?*

- *For whom should your direct mail appeal be written?*

- *How does this booklet compare with direct mail appeals your group has sent out?*

- *How does this booklet compare with other direct mail appeals you have seen?*

- *Which pages attracted your attention? Why?*

- *Where does your eye travel when you look at a page? Why?*

- *Did you read everything on each page, just the first and last sentences, or the sections in italics?*

- *Which techniques used in the booklet would be appropriate for your group's appeal letter? Why?*

SHARON PERCY ROCKEFELLER

Dear Friend:

Men run America.

Only 18 of the 435 members of the House of Representatives are women —about the same as 40 years ago.

None of the 100 United States Senators is a woman. In our entire history, there have only been 3 women elected to full Senate terms.

There are no women justices on the Supreme Court—and never have been.

Nationwide, women hold less than 7% of all elective offices.

After 200 years of public debate over equality, public office remains the fortress of inequality.

The perspective of 51.3% of the population is missing from government. More than unfair, this is a massive waste of energy and talent.

The Women's Campaign Fund is doing something about it. We're a national bi-partisan organization dedicated to helping capable, progressive women win public office.

We've already succeeded on a small scale. With your help, we can succeed on a large scale—and begin to turn the tide.

Please read about the Women's Campaign Fund in this booklet, and consider joining us by giving $25, or whatever you can afford.

Sincerely,

Sharon Percy Rockefeller

88

Half the Congress is missing.

Half the population—women—is barely represented in the Congress.

There are no women in the 100-member United States Senate. Only 18 of the 435 House members are women.

The imbalance is staggering—and nothing much has changed in 40 years.

One of the reasons is money. Elections usually hinge upon dollars spent.

Communicating with voters means television and radio time, newspaper space, printing, postage, personnel—hundreds of expenses and thousands of dollars. The candidate with the most exposure—which means the most money to purchase exposure—almost always wins.

It is a fact of political life that men find it easier than women to raise crucial campaign dollars.

If we don't try to change this, we're gambling with good government.

Women bring a unique and necessary perspective to lawmaking, a perspective the best-intentioned, most sensitive men simply cannot share. The experience of being female ought to be reflected in the activities of government.

Or it's only half a government.

After 200 Years:
Persons Who Have Served
In U.S. Government

	Men	Women
Senate	1,715	11
House	9,591	87
Supreme Court	101	0
Cabinet	507	5

Campaign contributions in 1976 by political action committees

AFL-CIO
$1,387,000

American
Medical
Association
$1,169,000

United
Automobile
Workers
$952,000

National
Association
of Realtors
$717,000

Associated
Milk
Producers
Inc.
$710,000

National
Education
Association
$616,000

Women's
Campaign
Fund
$63,000

Women Candidates:

☐ spend less than men. ☐ raise less than men.
☐ frighten political pros. ☐ lose due to lack of money.

All of the above.

It's a vicious psychological circle: Lack of money . . . leads to . . . losing the election . . . leads to . . . "Women can't win" syndrome . . . leads to . . . poor fund-raising . . . leads to . . . lack of money.

Party chieftains, wary of new-comers like women, spread the can't-win message. Scarce dollars become scarcer.

Gloria Schaffer, Connecticut's Secretary of State and a 1976 candidate for the U.S. Senate, says:

"Funds are just harder to raise for women. . . . Money has probably been the major reason why women have not been in the ballpark as far as running for higher office is concerned."

That's exactly why the Women's Campaign Fund was started.

In 1974, a small group of women and men set out to help women candidates. Operating at first with borrowed money, they managed to contribute $20,000 to women candidates—Democrats and Republicans—around the country. Seventeen of them won, and the organization grew.

In 1976, the Fund attracted 7,000 donors, contributed $63,000 and chalked up winners in 29 federal and state races.

It supported women running against anti-ERA state legislators as well as women in state and local races of special significance.

But, as the chart on the opposite page shows, it takes money. Too many close races have been lost because too few dollars were available.

To elect more women in 1978—to crack the can't-win syndrome—the Fund needs to triple its support.

It needs yours.

A good 2 month campaign takes a good 2 years.

A day late and a dollar short. That's the story of most women's campaigns—and that's why the Women's Campaign Fund is already working on the 1978 elections.

And it's working differently this time—by hand-picking vulnerable districts where women can win, recruiting good candidates (many of whom have held local office), providing them with nuts-and-bolts advice as well as dollars.

It's planning, preparation and practical politics.

What it means is that the Fund's 1978 dollars will go further than ever. Professional campaign advisers—working at bargain rates—will help plan and organize the selected campaigns. For every $1 the Fund spends in this way, women candidates will get $2 worth of services.

One thing isn't different, though. The money must be raised to make it all happen.

Please think about giving. A good campaign depends upon a good start now.

Candidates receiving financial assistance from the WCF are selected from among those women who have:

■ *a progressive stand on issues affecting the quality of life and human needs, a demonstrated commitment to establishment of a more just society, and a recognition of the concerns of women in the process of social change.*

■ *the ability to conduct a vigorous, professional campaign with a realistic chance of winning.*

■ *a need for financial help and/or campaign services.*

Helping Martha Keys find ways and means.

In 1974, the Women's Campaign Fund thought Martha Keys would be a good Congresswoman and contributed $1,500 to her campaign.

She defeated four men in the primary and went on to win the general election.

And she lived up to expectations. As the only woman on the powerful Ways and Means Committee, she pushed hard for tax reform, energy conservation and other important measures.

But re-election in 1976 wasn't easy. Her remarriage (to Indianapolis Congressman Andy Jacobs) led some to ask how she could represent her Kansas District while married to an Indiana Congressman. (Interestingly, no one asked Andy Jacobs the reverse question.)

The race heated up. The Fund put up $3,500, one of Martha's largest contributions, and urged others to help. It was close, but Martha won.

"The Women's Campaign Fund is making its mark on the Congress through its support of women candidates," Martha says. "As a survivor of a tight Congressional race myself, I know how crucial such support can be."

The Fund helped other Congresswomen withstand strong 1976 challenges—Shirley Chisholm (N.Y.), Helen Meyner (N.J.), Pat Schroeder (Col.) and Gladys Spellman (Md.).

Like Martha Keys on Ways and Means, these women hold major committee positions. Often alone.

The only way to change this is to elect more women.

Help us help them. Help more women find ways and means.

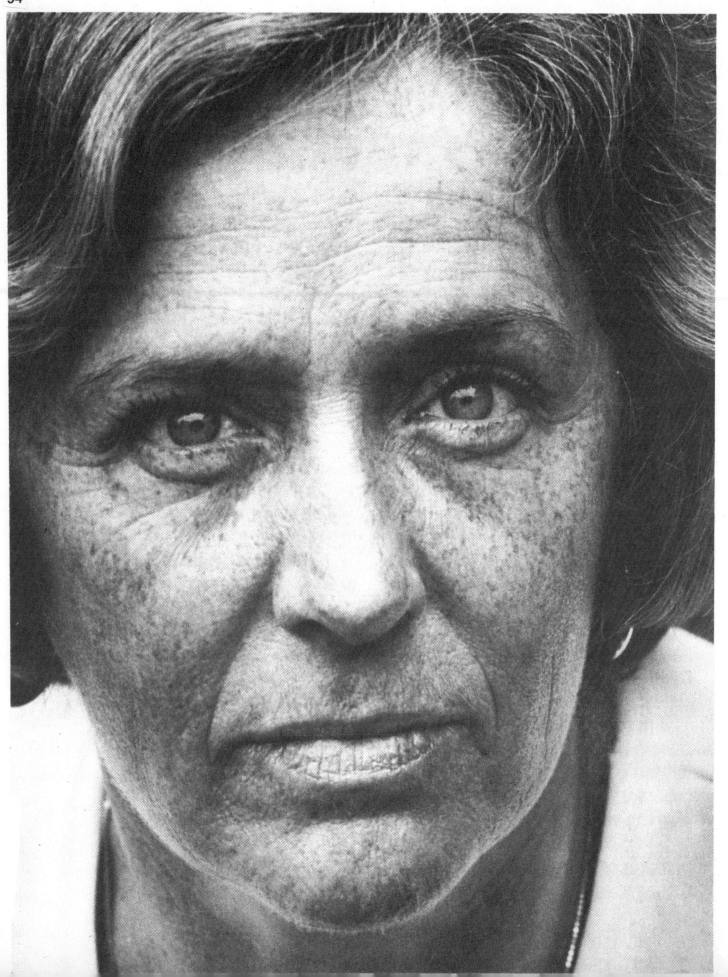

The other energy crisis.

Waste.

Waste of energy, waste of talent—because half the country isn't helping run the country.

Less than 7% of America's elected officials are women.

The sad part is that women have a lot to contribute. They could make a difference—because there *is* a difference between women and men.

Women view things from a unique perspective, shaped by their experience of life as women.

Their view of health needs and welfare reform is different.

They oppose wasteful military spending.

More than men, they experience the discrimination of income and inheritance taxes.

Women aren't all alike, of course. They wouldn't vote in a bloc. But their points of view would bring lawmaking into balance.

Not because they're the better half; because they're the other half.

One political scientist says: "I never met a woman in office who didn't feel she had to be more effective, more successful, more dedicated, more responsible, more moral, more everything, in order to be taken seriously."

Being taken seriously begins with winning elections—and winning elections begins with enough money to fight on equal ground.

Help the Women's Campaign Fund help elect some good women.

In this energy crisis, your dollars won't be wasted.

> *"Is there so great a superfluity of men fit for high duties, that society can afford to reject the service of any competent person? Are we so certain of always finding a man . . . for any duty or function of social importance which falls vacant, that we lose nothing by putting a ban upon one-half of mankind, and refusing beforehand to make their faculties available, however distinguished they may be.....?"*
>
> —John Stuart Mill,
> "The Subjection of Women,"
> 1869.

96

A Few Words.

Barbara Mikulski, Democratic Congresswoman from Maryland who received a $2,000 WCF contribution in 1976:

"Your contribution came when money from other sources was running low. It permitted us to buy early radio spots that convinced contributors and the news media we were running a serious and potentially successful campaign. Thank you for being there when you were most needed."

Norma Paulus, Republican Secretary of State and the first woman elected to statewide Constitutional office in Oregon:

"Your $1,000 contribution helped put a solid financial base under my general election campaign."

Morris Udall, Congressman from Arizona:

"For every woman elected to public office there are 13 men. In the Congress the ratio is 30 to one. The Women's Campaign Fund is trying to do something about this outrage, and it deserves assistance and support."

Earleen Collins, who defeated a Daley-backed, anti-ERA candidate to become the first black woman to serve in the Illinois State Senate:

"[Your contribution] gave all of us the lift we needed at a very difficult time. . . . All of the generous people who contributed to the Women's Campaign Fund can be very proud. . . . Our victory is looked on as an historic accomplishment."

Edward Brooke, Senator from Massachusetts:

"There ought to be many, many more women in public office. The waste of talent is simply a crime. I hope women will run and win—we need them."

Write us in and write it off.

Your contribution to the Women's Campaign Fund is tax-deductible—or you can take a tax credit.

```
(Form 1040)
Part IV   Credits
48  Credit for the elderly (attach Schedules R & RP) . . . . . 48
49  Credit for child care expenses (attach Form 2441) . . . . 49
50  Investment credit (attach Form 3468) . . . . . . . . . . 50
51  Foreign tax credit (attach Form 1116) . . . . . . . . . 51
52  Contributions to candidates for public office credit (see page 12 of Instructions) . . . 52
53  Work Incentive (WIN) Credit (attach Form 4874) . . . . . 53

Miscellaneous Deductions (See page 15 of Instructions.)

30  Alimony paid . . . . . . . .
31  Union dues . . . . . . . . .
32  Other (itemize) ▶
```

We'll use the money to support progressive women leaders who have a solid chance to win—and who need the dollars.

And, in 1978, we'll buy professional campaign help at half price. Our candidates will get more for your money.

In the past, even our limited funds made a difference. We've supported 46 winners, including Congresswomen Elizabeth Holtzman (New York), Yvonne Burke (California), Millicent Fenwick (New Jersey), Barbara Jordan (Texas) and Shirley Pettis (California).

In 1976, we helped elect the first woman to hold statewide constitutional office in Oregon—Secretary of State Norma Paulus. And we helped 20 pro-ERA women win legislative seats in unratified states.

In 1978, though, we have to do a lot better.

We want more victories—so women can stop looking in and start pitching in.

Will you buy in?

Changing Times

Gallup Poll responses to the question, Would you support a woman for President?

1937	31%	yes
1970	53%	yes
1975	73%	yes

(The Gallup Poll also reports that 7 of 10 Americans think the country would be better governed if more women held public office.)

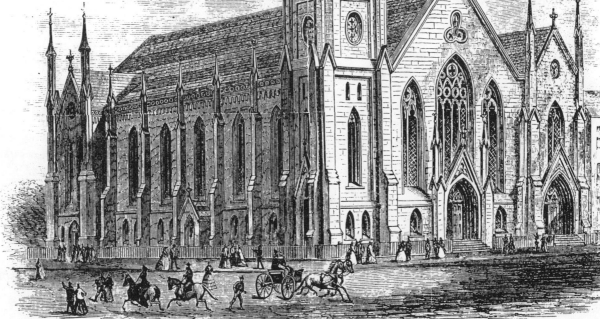

The Habit of Giving: Church Funding

Of all the "private" sources of funding, churches are more apt to take "risks" and support activities that attempt to empower the poor. Food and nutrition programs, prison reform, Vietnam-era veterans, community organizing, self-help projects, migrant farmworkers and many others have received funding from various churches. Some issues citizen groups need to keep in mind are:

- **Churches are not required to report their contributions.** Because of this, data on church-giving is limited and there is no clearinghouse of information as there is for foundations (The Foundation Center) and government funding (Office of Management and Budget). Some of the church-sponsored funds do publish application guidelines and names of past grant recipients, but the initial task of the fundraiser is to determine who in the church hierarchies is responsible for "nonsacramental activities."

Harper's
Weekly, 1869.

One approach is to identify the treasurer or finance person of local churches and ask them about the church's community service activities. Aside from local efforts, citizen groups should also ask about the church's regional and national funding offices that have been established. Another option is to find out who among your group's membership belongs to local churches and ask them to approach church officials.

- **Churches vary widely in structure.** Each denomination handles its funding expenditures differently. One can assume, however, that contributions are often made at the local parish level, sometimes regionally and nationally.

Again, community groups should begin at the local level and work their way up through the hierarchy of the church. One critical question to ask is who ultimately approves all grants. The purpose of this is to clarify the decision-makers process and personally contact decision-makers when possible.

Some of the national funds established to help poor people are listed below.

Church	Related Fund
• Presbyterian Church	National Committee on the Self-Development of People; Ghetto Loan and Investment Committee
• Catholic Church	Campaign for Human Development
• United Church of Christ	Committee on Racial Justice; Office of Communications
• Methodist Church	Fund for Reconciliation; Fund for Religion and Race
• Episcopal Church	Community Action and Human Development; Economic Development Corporation
• Ecumenical	Interreligious Foundation for Community Organization

- **Churches don't have to give to 501 (C)(3) organizations.** Although some churches do insist that grantees be nonprofit and tax-exempt, they are not legally required to restrict grants to 501 (C)(3) organizations.

- **Certain denominations take specific stands on an issue.** The obvious example is the Catholic Church's stand on abortion and birth control. Citizen groups are cautioned to investigate religious beliefs on controversial issues prior to submitting a proposal.

Discussion Questions:

- *In what ways could your group work more closely with local churches? Have you talked with them about how to approach churches for funding?*

- *What strategies could you use to approach a local church?*

- *Why would a church or church-sponsored fund be interested in your organization?*

Gone With The Wind: Federal Funding

"Awesome, too bureaucratic, complicated, too much red tape, highly competitive"—these are some typical comments about federal funding. The world of federal funding is surrounded by fact, fiction and lots of confusion. This introduction includes some very basic information; readers are encouraged to talk with experienced fundraisers and consult the many articles on federal funding in the **Grantsmanship Center News.**

What Are the Origins of Federal Assistance Programs?

Assistance programs begin in Congress. Congress acts on proposed legislation and, if passed, the legislation authorizes new grant programs. The original legislation is often significantly modified or dies a quiet death during the Congressional review process, so applicants should attempt to follow relevant bills as they progress through Congress.

Appropriation of funds for grant programs is an entirely separate process, however it is also a Congressional responsibility. The annual budget prepared by the President plays an important role in determining federal spending priorities. Once the proposed budget is submitted to Congress, a long and complicated process begins.

The federal agency responsible for administering assistance programs develops regulations and guidelines and publishes them in the **Federal Register.** Comments on the proposed regulations are solicited and final regulations appear in the **Federal Register.**

In short, there are three aspects of the federal assistance process that applicants should follow—specific legislation, the US budget, and program regulations.

What Types of Assistance Does the Federal Government Provide?

1. **Categorical Grants:** The 450 categorical grants listed in the **Catalog of Federal Domestic Assistance** are collectively the largest source of federal assistance for state and local governments and non profit fit organizations. There are four types of categorical grants:

   • *Project Grants:* The nearly 300 project grants are awarded on a competitive basis by the administering federal agency. Applications must be submitted for specific projects adhering to the regulations published in the **Federal Register.**

   • *Formula-Project Grants:* These grants are awarded to states based on uniform allocation formulas and are awarded within the states on a competitive basis.

   • *Formula-Apportioned Grants:* Criteria spelled out in the authorizing legislation or regulations are used to establish the formula by which these grants are awarded.

   • *Open-Ended Reimbursement:* This type of assistance is used to reimburse state and local governments for a portion of the costs of running specific programs, like the Aid for Dependent Children Program.

2. **Block Grants:** The most widely known block grant program is the Comprehensive Employment and Training Act (CETA) which replaced several categorical manpower training programs. The intent of

block grants is to provide states with more flexible monies than those available from categorical grant programs. However, by the time the funds filter down to local governments and nonprofit organizations, many regulations have usually restricted the use of the funds to specific types of projects.

3. **General Revenue-Sharing:** Revenue-sharing monies are automatically distributed to state and local governments. The uses of revenue sharing funds have been widely criticized in the past—citizen groups should attend public hearings in their communities where local spending priorities are established.

4. **Non-financial Assistance:** Some of the programs in the **Catalog of Federal Domestic Assistance** involve technical assistance rather than direct financial aid. In addition to technical assistance, some nonprofit groups are eligible to buy surplus government property (desks, chairs, filing cabinets, etc.) at very reasonable prices. Check with the US General Services Administration (Business Service Center) in your region to find out if your group is eligible.

Because so much federal money is now "flowing through" state governments, citizen groups would be wise to establish contacts with appropriate state agencies and with county and local government officials. Maintaining contacts with state legislators is yet another source of information on funding programs passed by state legislatures.

The process of applying for public sector funding is long and tedious. Even so, many nonprofit groups have successfully written federal grant applications. One of the major frustrations with public sector funding is that it's "trendy." Funding for day care, for example, reached its peak in the early 1970s and has since been reduced. Funding for programs serving the elderly is now "in." So, for citizen groups who are contemplating applying for public sector funding, it would be prudent to think about the future of the program. If groups can answer this one critical question—What will happen once the federal money runs out?—the chances of survival are much greater.

ber for grant programs you think are appropriate for your organization is important, since your requests for information will undoubtedly require the Catalog number. Programs in the Catalog are arranged in numerical order; so, for example, number 10.203 will appear at the beginning of the Catalog and 64.107 will appear near the end.

There are eight indices in the Catalog and each one is described in the introduction entitled "How to Use the Catalog." The most important one is the Subject Index. Users should look under several topics because the Office of Management and Budget's descriptive words may not coincide with your own. For example, "organizing" and "social change" don't appear in the index and "minorities" has only three programs listed.

Once you've jotted down the numbers of programs that sound relevant, refer to the Program Description section. A sample program description and explanation of contents follows. Some questions you might want to keep in mind while analyzing the program descriptions are:

"President Ford and the Congress have worked out a compromise on spending priorities -- we don't get lunch but every day at noon they pass out pictures of Trident submarines and B-1 bombers."

Researching Federal Funding

Federal funding information fits better into a wheelbarrow than a folder. The initial problem for citizen groups is to wade through all the material and select relevant funding programs. This section deals with how to identify government funding possibilities.

1. **Catalog of Federal Domestic Assistance ($18/year)**
    Superintendent of Documents
    Government Printing Office
    Washington, D.C. 20402

Compiled by the Office of Management and Budget, the Catalog lists details on over 1,000 federal assistance programs—those that provide grants, technical assistance, and loans for which applications must be submitted. Because of the latter restriction, general revenue-sharing doesn't appear in the Catalog because state and local governments automatically receive revenue-sharing funds.

Each program in the Catalog is identified with a five-digit number. Knowing the identifying num-

- *Is your agency eligible to receive funding from this program?*
- *Do the objectives of the program seem compatible with those of your organization?*
- *Are there any restrictions on how the funds can be used?*
- *Is this a matching grant?*
- *Have appropriations for this program been increasing or decreasing in recent years?*
- *Who can you contact for more information?*

A detailed description of how to analyze the Catalog's contents appears in a **Grantsmanship Center News** reprint, *How to Use the Catalog of Federal Domestic Assistance* (1015 West Olympic Boulevard, Los Angeles, CA 90015, $1.25).

104

Federal Assistance Programs Retrieval System (FAPRS)

Rural Development Service
Department of Agriculture
14th and Independence Avenues
Washington, D.C. 20250

FAPRS is a computerized shortcut to browsing through the indices of the **Catalog of Federal Domestic Assistance.** Begun in 1975 by the Rural Development Service, the computer system is now being transferred to the Office of Management and Budget, which also prepares the **Catalog of Federal Domestic Assistance.** Because the system and authorizing legislation are so new, FAPRS is not yet perfect, but the potential for saving time is real.

The major criticism of the present system is that the categories are too broad. There are eight major categories (social services, health, employment, etc.) and 82 subcategories. Users may select one or more of the subcategories for a fee of $5 per subcategory. The result will be the names of relevant federal assistance programs and the Catalog's five digit identifying numbers.

In spite of its shortcomings, fundraisers new to the federal funding scene may find FAPRS a useful starting point. It still is necessary to use the Catalog and contact the federal agency for more information, but FAPRS will provide an initial list of relevant assistance programs.

To locate a terminal near you, contact the Rural Development Service at the address above. In Massachusetts, contact Community Resource Development Program, Department of Food and Resource Economics, University of Massachusetts, Amherst, MA 01003, (413) 545-2496, or your local county extension office.

The Federal Register ($50/year)

Superintendent of Documents
Government Printing Office
Washington, D.C. 20402

Published weekdays, the **Federal Register** includes proposed and final regulations for federal grant programs, deadlines for submitting applications, criteria for how applications will be reviewed and much more. It's advisable to skim the Register every day or consult the indices which usually appear in April and October. "Governmentese," the government's own version of the English language, is another feature which runs throughout the Register.

Commerce Business Daily ($75/year)

Superintendent of Documents
Government Printing Office
Washington, D.C. 20402

Prepared by the Department of Commerce, the **Commerce Business Daily** (CBD) is another weekday publication, infamous as the most boring and incomprehensible government publication. In spite of its deficiencies, CBD does contain useful information on contract opportunities for nonprofit (and for profit) organizations.

Government purchase of services, equipment, materials, and research must go through a bidding process and bidding "invitations" appear in CBD. Potential contracts advertised in CBD cover very specific services that the government wants to buy.

The entries in CBD are sure to be bewildering, especially if you've missed the Monday issue. Many entries say "see note 8" and search as you may, "note 8" is nowhere to be found. These "numbered notes" are contained in Monday's issue and are *not* repeated in the issues for the remainder of the week.

Contract opportunities for which nonprofit groups are eligible are found in the first part, called "Services." Under the "Services" category, relevant sections for nonprofit groups are:

1. Section A: Experimental, Developmental, Test and Research Work (including basic and applied research)

2. Section H: Expert and Consultant Services

3. Section U: Training

If the entry says, "RFP Available," then applicants should write to the agency asking for a copy of the RFP (Request for Proposal). The RFP contains a description of the work to be done under the contract, an approximate timetable, and criteria for how the proposals will be evaluated. If the entry asks for qualifications, applicants should submit statements of their experience and capabilities. RFPs will then be sent only to organizations that have the necessary qualifications.

Another option is to submit statements of qualifications and request that the organization be placed on the mailing list to receive RFPs when they become available.

Another section in CBD, "Contract Awards," lists recipients of federal contracts of $25,000 or more. Some organizations call contract recipients to explore the possibility of subcontracting. Surplus government property appears at the end of the issue, listing everything from beds to computer software (consumable supplies are *not* included) and can be a source of inexpensive materials for nonprofit organizations.

Other Sources of Information

U.S. Government Manual ($6.50/year)
Superintendent of Documents
Government Printing Office
Washington, D.C. 20402

Published annually by the Office of the Federal Register, the Manual is indispensable. It covers the legislative, judicial, and executive branches. It's helpful, for example, in determining the structure of the Department of Health, Education and Welfare or in finding the names and titles of key agency personnel. One section, the Guide to Boards, Committees, and Commissions, lists the names and addresses of a variety of panels and boards that were set up by Congress or the President. Some, such as the National Clearinghouse on Aging, can provide useful information to groups working in a particular subject area.

Code of Federal Regulations
Superintendent of Documents
Government Printing Office
Washington, D.C. 20402

One important piece of information for grant-seekers are the regulations that apply to each assistance program. Much more detailed than the information in the **Catalog**, the Code (CFR) contain specific objectives for the program, an explanation of the application process and how proposals will be evaluated, and information on what costs are "allowable" under the program. Published first in the **Federal Register**, the regulations are compiled into the Code by topic area. Thus, when you see a reference in the **Catalog of Federal Domestic Assistance** in the "Regulations, Guidelines and Literature" section of the program description, you can order the appropriate volume from the nearest federal bookstore.

Federal Agencies

Establishing contacts with people in federal agencies is critical. Some fundraisers make periodic visits to Washington to meet with staff people to get information and to "get known." Some bring along "walking papers," which give a brief background on their organization and a summary of future plans, to discuss with staffpeople in different federal agencies. Another option is to make frequent phone calls to federal agency staff, asking for information about recent developments, new programs, funding priorities, etc.

Most federal agencies also publish voluminous materials about their assistance programs. Publications offices for each agency are listed in the **U.S. Government Manual**. You can ask for a publications list and ask to be put on the agency's mailing list to receive free publications.

The purpose of any of the above is (1) to get general information about the federal agency, (2) to make contact with individuals in agencies who can be called or visited periodically for information, (3) to get referrals to other appropriate agencies, and (4) to let administrative people know you exist, what you do, and what kind of funding or assistance you need.

One experienced fundraiser suggests that prospective applicants ask *specific* questions and be as brief as possible in describing their organizations—"talking less and listening more." Applicants should also collect as much written information as possible from the federal agency and keep copious notes on all visits and conversations.

If you've identified a federal grant program then a phone call or visit to the agency is necessary to get the application form, regulations and guidelines for the program. One common mistake is that groups often struggle with the application form and send it in without consulting the agency. It's better to call the agency with *any* questions you have, rather than submit an incorrect application.

Congressional Offices

It's necessary to keep in touch with your U.S. Senators and Representatives. Some are quite helpful in suggesting possible funding sources. If you should apply for federal funding, send a copy of the proposal to your Congresspeople.

Federal Management Circulars and Office of Management and Budget Circulars

In the past, each federal agency developed its own administrative requirements for grants. The result was that a grant-seeker had to be familiar with a wide variety of requirements issued by each federal agency.

An effort to simplify federal grant policies began in 1969. It resulted in a series of "uniform standards" that are now being used by many federal agencies. The circulars cover such topics as what costs can be included in application budgets, the process for revising budgets, how indirect costs are determined, and

Similar to FMC 74-7, **this is the most important circular for non-profit groups.** Included is a widely used standard application form (SF 424). Also included are matching share requirements, financial management and reporting requirements, and more.

OMB Circular A-95, revised: **Evaluation, Review, and Coordination of Federal and Federally Assisted Programs and Projects, January 13, 1976**

Reprinted from Workforce

what kind of financial management system an applicant must have.

A summary of circulars relevant to citizen groups is listed below. It's advisable to have a copy of these circulars on hand because they're referred to frequently in the **Catalog of Federal Domestic Assistance** and other federal publications. Free copies of the circulars may be ordered from:

Publications Office
Office of Management and Budget
726 Jackson Place, N.W.
Washington, D.C. 20503
(202) 395-4660

OMB Circular A-110: **Uniform Administrative Requirements for Grants and Agreements with Institutions of Higher Education, Hospitals and other Nonprofit Organizations, July 30, 1976**

Many federal funding applicants must now notify state and area-wide clearinghouses *prior* to sending the applications to the federal agency. Programs that are subject to A-95 review are listed in an appendix in the **Catalog of Federal Domestic Assistance.** Applicants should also check with the federal agency responsible for specific programs to be certain whether or not the program they're applying for requires A-95 review.

OMB Circular A-111: **Jointly Funded Assistance to State and Local Governments and Nonprofit Organizations, July 30, 1976**

This circular describes the process of applying for funding from

several federal assistance programs.
Some federal assistance programs
have been designated as "eligible
for joint funding," this means
that applicants may submit one
application rather than a separate
application for each assistance
program. For example, the City
of Boston, Massachusetts, recently submitted "the Boston Plan,"
an application for federal assistance for job training, transportation, housing, and urban development *in one package.* The program descriptions in the **Catalog
of Federal Domestic Assistance**
indicate whether or not the assistance program is one that is "eligible for joint funding." To date,
cities have been recipients of
some joint funding, but nonprofits have not. This may change
in the future, though, as federal
agencies become more willing to
coordinate their funding, so nonprofits should be familiar with
the contents of Circular A-111.

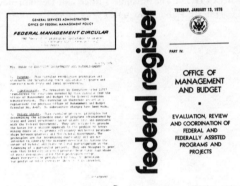

FMC 74-7:   **Uniform Administrative Requirements for Grants-in-Aid to State
and Local Governments,
September 13, 1974**

This circular appears frequently
in the **Catalog** even though it is
primarily aimed at grants for
state and local governments. Uniform standards for nonprofits are
covered by Circular A-110. But
because both FMC 74-4 and FMC
74-7 are referred to frequently,
it's helpful to be familiar with
them.

FMC 74-4:   **Cost Principles Applicable to
Grants and Contracts with State
and Local Governments,
July 18, 1974**

Covers rules for determining direct and indirect costs for state
and local government applications.

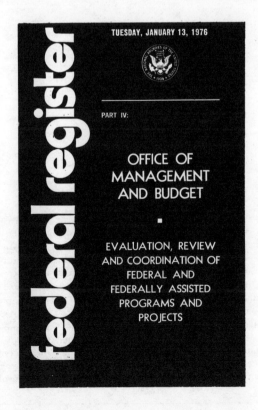

108

Sample Program Description from the Catalog of Federal Domestic Assistance

Key to Program Descriptions in the Catalog of Federal Domestic Assistance

13.623 ADMINISTRATION FOR CHILDREN, YOUTH AND FAMILIES–RUNAWAY YOUTH

FEDERAL AGENCY: OFFICE OF HUMAN DEVELOPMENT SERVICES, DEPARTMENT OF HEALTH, EDUCATION, AND WELFARE

The federal agency and subdivision responsible for the program are identified here. The specific office running the program is listed under "Information Contacts."

AUTHORIZATION: The Juvenile Justice and Delinquency Prevention Act, Title III; Public Law 93-415; 42 U.S.C. 5701, as amended.

This lists the law and amendments, if any, that authorize the assistance program. Reading the law is helpful in determining why the program was created. If the law has been amended recently, the changes may not be reflected in the Catalog, so applicants should find out from the federal agency whether or not amendments have been passed or new regulations issued.

OBJECTIVES: To develop local facilities to address the immediate needs of runaway youth.

If the government practiced what it preached, these objectives would be much more specific and helpful to prospective applicants. As it is, this will give you only a general idea of the purpose of the program.

TYPES OF ASSISTANCE: Project Grants.

The types of assistance are explained in the Catalog's introduction. Nonprofit organizations will be most interested in project grants (grants to organizations for specific projects) but should not disregard formula grants (made to state and local governments). Nonprofits may be able to subcontract with state and local governments to perform services funded under the federal program.

USES AND USE RESTRICTIONS: Grants are for (1) the establishment, and/or strengthening of an existing or proposed runaway house, a locally controlled facility providing temporary shelter, counseling and aftercare services to juveniles who have left home without permission of their parents or guardians; (2) and to otherwise homeless youth. JOINT FUNDING: This program is considered suitable for joint funding with closely related Federal financial assistance programs in accordance with the provisions of OMB Circular No. A-111. For programs that are not identified as suitable for joint funding, the applicant may consult the headquarters or field office of the appropriate funding agency for further information on statutory or other restrictions involved.

Usually more specific than "Objectives," this section tells you what grants can and cannot be used for.

This program is "eligible for joint funding." This means that an applicant may submit one application to be funded under this and other related assistance programs, rather than submitting a separate application to each program.

ELIGIBILITY REQUIREMENTS:

Applicant Eligibility: These grants are available to states, localities or nonprofit private agencies, or coordinated networks of such agencies.

Beneficiary Eligibility: Runaway youth and their families.

Credentials/Documentation: Proof of nonprofit status for private, nonprofit organizations. Applicable costs and administrative procedures will be determined in accordance with Part 74 of Title 45 of the Code of Federal Regulations, which implements the requirements of FMC 74-4.

APPLICATION AND AWARD PROCESS:

Preapplication Coordination: Applications are subject to State and areawide clearinghouses review pursuant to procedures in Part I, Attachment A of OMB Circular No. A-95 (revised). Consultation or assistance is available from the Youth Development Bureau, Office of Human Development Services, Department of Health, Education and Welfare. The standard application forms as furnished by the Federal agency and required by OMB Circular A-102 must be used for this program.

Application Procedure: Application kits may be obtained from the ACYF Regional Office. This program is subject to the provisions of OMB Circular No. A-110.

Award Procedure: The Director ACYF Unit in the Regional Office in consultation with the Director, Youth Development Bureau or an appointed designee approves or rejects individual applications. Notification of awards must be made to the designated State Central Information Reception Agency in accordance with Treasury Circular 1082.

Who's eligible to receive funding and who should benefit from the program are included in this section.

"Proof of nonprofit status" consists of the organization's letter from the Internal Revenue Service which says that it is tax exempt under Section 501 (C)(3) of the IRS Code and "not a private foundation" under Section 509 (A)(1,2, or 3) of the Code. Federal Management Circular 74-4 is described later in this chapter.

*This section describes what must be done before a formal application is submitted. The most important thing to look for is whether or not the application must go through the A-95 review process. If it does, applications must be submitted to area and state clearinghouses **prior** to submission to the federal agency. The purpose of A-95 is to give state and local government officials the opportunity to comment on applications. Although clearinghouse recommendations are only advisory, federal agencies are likely to scrutinize applications with negative comments quite carefully. One major consideration for applicants is to allow more time, since clearinghouses can take up to 30 days (or longer if issues need to be negotiated) to comment on applications. Applicants should contact A-95 clearinghouses in their state for more information (listed in an appendix to the Catalog of Federal Domestic Assistance). In Massachusetts, the state clearinghouse is the Commonwealth of Massachusetts Office of State Planning.*

Because this section on the application process is usually brief, applicants should always call the federal agency for more details.

The office responsible for making funding decisions is listed here. Applicants should contact this office with questions on how to fill out the application, etc. For example, if the decisions are made in Washington, it's advisable to call Washington with your questions rather than the regional office to minimize the chance of being given misinformation. In this example, the decision is made

Deadlines: As specified in the announcement or application instructions.

Range of Approval/Disapproval Time: 60 to 90 days.

Appeals: Applicants will be notified by letter on grant refusals. Applicants may appeal adverse decision to the DHEW Grant Appeals Board. Instructions on appeals are available from the Regional Office.

Renewals: Requests for renewal (continuation grant) are handled in the same manner as an original grant. No grant is automatically approved for more than 1 year.

ASSISTANCE CONSIDERATIONS:

Formula and Matching Requirements: Federal share of grant is up to 90 percent. The non-Federal share may be in cash or in-kind.

Length and Time Phasing of Assistance: Grant awards are made for 1 year only. The award is issued in the total amount approved. Payments are made monthly to the grantee. Total length of project will not exceed 3 years.

POST ASSISTANCE REQUIREMENTS:

Reports: Financial and program reports annually; monthly data on clients served; final reports are required 90 days after termination of project.

Audits: All project activities are subject to audit.

Records: All financial records are to be maintained 3 years after termination of the project or until audit is completed, whichever occurs first.

FINANCIAL INFORMATION:

Account Identification: 75-1636-0-1-500.

Obligations: (Grants) FY 77 $7,998,000; FY 78 est $11,000,000; and FY 79 est $11,000,000.

Range and Average of Financial Assistance: $25,000 to $75,000; $68,000.

---

at the regional level, so questions should be directed there.

Although knowing the deadline for submitting the application is obviously critical, the Catalog rarely indicates specific dates. Checking the Federal Register or calling the federal agency are the two primary ways of finding out when applications are due.

Many federal grants require that a portion of the total cost of a project come from other sources. This is called a "matching share" or "cost-sharing." In the example to the left, the federal government will pay 90% of the project costs. The remaining 10% can be cash contributions from other sources or in-kind (non-money) donations from the applicant or other sources such as office space or volunteers.

What this says here is that applicants can submit one-year proposals, although grants may be renewed using the same application process. It also tells you when payments are made. In this case, they are made monthly. It does not say, however, if funds are to be advanced or if costs will be reimbursed at the end of the month. Again, a call to the federal agency is appropriate to determine how and when the grant will be paid.

Be sure to get copies of all required reporting forms before the project begins. In this sample annual reports are required; but you should look them over to determine what kind of information needs to be collected during the project.

Determining the amount of funds available is an important piece of information for fundraisers, but unfortunately, the Catalog doesn't include it. The Catalog does note how much money was spent in previous years and an estimate for the current fiscal year. You can look for trends with this information, such as the general increase or decline in funds. Because the financial information in the Catalog is indequate (and often inaccurate), applicants should contact

PROGRAM ACCOMPLISHMENTS: Awarded 128 grants totaling $7,998,000 during fiscal year 1977. These projects will serve approximately 39,000 runaway youth in 44 states; Puerto Rico, Guam, and the District of Columbia.

REGULATIONS, GUIDELINES, AND LITERATURE: Regulations for the Runaway Youth Program (45 CFR, Part 1351), annual program announcements are available form the ACYF regional offices.

INFORMATION CONTACTS:
Regional or Local Office: Contact, Director, Children, Youth and Families Division, Office of Human Development Services Regional Offices.
Headquarters Office: Director, Youth Development Bureau, Administration for Children, Youth and Families, Office of Human Development Services, Department of Health, Education, and Welfare, Washington, DC 20201. Telephone: (202) 245-2870.

RELATED PROGRAMS: 13.242, Mental Health Research Grants; 13.430, Educationally Deprived Children-State Administration; 13.608, Administration for Children, Youth and Families-Child Welfare Research and Demonstration; 16.005, Public Education on Drug Abuse-Technical Assistance; 16.500, Law Enforcement Assistance-Comprehensive Planning Grants; 13.810, Public Assistance-State and Local Training; 16.503, Law Enforcement Assistance-Technical Assistance.

---

the federal agency to find out how much money is currently available for the program. NOTE: "TQ" means transitional quarter, the period during which the federal government's fiscal year was changed from July 1 to October 1.

The types of projects that have been funded in the past are described in "Program Acc Accomplishments," sometimes with considerable detail or, as in this sample, very minimally.

Regulations for federal assistance programs spell out requirements, application deadlines, criteria for how the proposals will be reviewed, and other necessary information. Regulations are first published in the **Federal Register,** *then compiled in the Code of Federal Regulations. In this example, "45 CFR Part 1351" refers to Volume 45 of the Code of Federal Regulations, Part 1351. Copies of individual volumes may be purchased at government bookstores. Often, other literature is mentioned in this section and applicants should read it all. There may be other literature not mentioned in the Catalog so applicants should collect everything the federal agency has that sounds relevant to the program.*

This section gives you the names of offices to contact at the regional and national levels. The **US Government Manual** *can supplement this with the names of individuals to contact in these offices.*

"Related Programs" section is not complete, but it's always worth looking at the program descriptions.

Commerce Business Daily

U. S. DEPARTMENT OF COMMERCE
Juanita M. Kreps, Secretary

A daily list of U.S. Government procurement invitations, contract awards, subcontracting leads, sales of surplus property and foreign business opportunities

U. S. GOVERNMENT PROCUREMENTS

Services

A Experimental, Developmental, Test and Research Work (includes both basic and applied research).

A -- STATEMENT OF CAPABILITIES FOR INVESTIGATIONS INTO THE TOXICOLOGICAL EFFECTS OF POLYBROMINATED BIPHENYLS (PBB's) on Michigan Farmers and Chemical Workers. The National Institute of Environmental Health Sciences is seeking organizations capable of performing investigations into the toxicological effects of PBB's on Michigan farmers and chemical workers. Interested organizations must have these capabilities. (1) Assured access to the following groups of individuals: (a) About 500 residents and consumers from farms quarantined as a result of an episode of inadvertent contamination to farm feed with PBB's in place of magnesium oxide in the preparation of a special feed supplement for lactating cows in Michigan in 1973; (b) About 500 control residents and consumers from non-quanrantined area farms; (c) About 50 workers employed in the Michigan Chemical Company plant which manufactured the PBB's; and (d) About 250 control farmers and members of their families from an adjacent state with no known similar episode of PBB exposure. (2) Ability to investigate over a three-year period serial changes (or absence of changes) in these groups using 1976-1977 baseline findings for comparison with regard to neurological status, liver function, arthritis-like changes, immunological status, and body burden of PBB's. The NIEHS intends to negotiate a sole source contract with The Mount Sinai Medical Center, New York, New York, under the direction of Dr. George G. Bekesi, if other organizations having the same capabilities cannot be identified. This is not a request for proposals. Responses should not include cost of pricing information. Concise responses directed specifically to the points mentioned above are requested. Resumes of all key personnel shall be provided as well as a description of the facilities and equipment available. NIEHS will carefully evaluate all responses. An RFP will be sent to qualified organizations. Unqualified organizations will be so notified in order to save them the expense and effort of submitting proposals. It should be noted, however, that this procedure does not preclude any organization from requesting an RFP and submitting a proposal. Responses must reference RFP No. NIH-ES-78-2. Four (4) copies of the response must be received on or before COB 24 Jul 78. (173)

Procurement Office, National Institute of Environmental Health Sciences, Attn: W. R. Johnston, Bldg. 11, Room 1101, P.O. Box 12233, Research Triangle Park, NC 27709

A -- DESIGN, FABRICATION AND TESTING OF THE FEASIBILITY OF APPLYING SQUEEZE CASTING TECHNIQUES in the fabrication of munitions metal parts. Propose to procure by negotiation services for the above from Illinois Institute of Technology Research Institute, Chicago, Illinois. RFP DAAK10-78-R-0097. Contact is R. Glanowski, DRDAR-PRW-A, Tel. 201/328-3272. See Note 46. (165)

US Army Armament R&D Command, Dover, NJ 07801

A -- STUDY OF THE INCIDENCED OF DRUGS AMONG FATALLY INJURED DRIVERS to determine to what extent drugs are detected in fatally injured drivers and the similarity to other drivers. Closing date 13 Jul 78. OML Code 0.122. Notes 64 and 80 apply. (166)

Department of Transportation, National Highway Traffic Safety Admin., Office of Contracts and Procurement, 400 Seventh Street, S.W., Washington, DC 20590

SINGLE WEEKLY LISTING OF ALL THE NUMBERED NOTES

The 'Numbered Notes' will be published only on the first working day of each week. As in today's issue, all the active 'Numbered Notes' are contained on the last three pages. These pages should be retained for reference during the current week.

For extra copies of or assistance with the 'Notes' contact the COMMERCE BUSINESS DAILY, Rm. 1304, 433 W. Van Buren St., Chicago, IL 60607; Tel: 312/353-2950.

A -- TECHNICAL SUPPORT FOR THE DEVELOPMENT OF INFORMATION AND RECOMMENDATIONS—regarding medium and heavy truck noise regulations. Seek a contractor who is knowledgeable in manufacturing and operation of medium and heavy trucks to provide the EPA's Noise Enforcement Division with the necessary technical expertise on medium and heavy trucks and the truck industry that is necessary to resolve issues arising in the course of enforcement of newly regulated medium and heavy trucks. The contractor must possess a working knowledge of both the foreign and domestic truck industry. He must also have the working knowledge of noise emission aspects of trucks. Requests must be issued in writing. Please ask for RFP WA 78-C223 and state your EPA ''RFP List'' number if you have been assigned one. See Note 24.

A -- TECHNICAL SUPPORT SERVICES—on the manufacture and operation of portable air compressors. These services will provide the EPA's Noise Enforcement Division with the necessary technical expertise on portable air compressors that is necessary to ensure that newly regulated portable air compressors comply with the noise emission standard. The Contractor must possess a detailed knowledge of the functional characteristics of the individual compressor components, the operation and manufacturing techniques commonly used by the industry to produce portable air compressors.. Requests must be issued in writing. Please ask for RFP WA 78-C224 and state your EPA 'RFP List' number is you have been assigned one. See Note 24.

🌑 A -- COST AND ECONOMIC ANALYSIS—of Industrial Machines. Requirement for nonpersonal contractual services to provide an economic profile of industrial machinery affected by noise emission regulations. Requests must be issued in writing. Please ask for RFP WA 78-C297 and state your EPA 'RFP List' number if you have been assigned one. See Note 24. (165)

EPA, Headquarters Contract Operations, Contracts Support Section, Contract Preparation Unit (PM-214-C), Crystal Mall #2, Room 708, Washington, DC 20460

★ A -- ADDITIONAL SUPPORT to the Long Range Acoustic Propagation Project (LRAPP) concerning the improvement, maintenance and documentation of acoustic models. Negotiations conducted with Ocean Data Systems, Inc., 6000 Executive Blvd., Rockville, MD 20852. See Note 46.

★ A -- ADDITIONAL EVALUATION and development of decision aiding technologies. Negotiations conducted with Applied Psychological Services, Inc., Science Center, Wayne, PA 19087. See Note 46.

★ A -- ADDITIONAL RESEARCH in monolithically integrated FETs and TEDs for gigabit shift register. Negotiations conducted with Hughes Research Laboratories, 3011 Malibu Canyon Rd., Malibu, CA 90265. See Note 46.

★ A -- ANALYTICAL SERVICES to review and update the Preliminary Coordination in Direct Support (CIDS) Exercise Analysis Guide using lessons learned developed during initial attempts to apply the methodology in Fleet exercises. Negotiations conducted with Atlantic Analysis Corporation, 5 Koger Executive Center, Suite 219, Norfolk, VA 23502. See Note 46.

★ A -- LIFTING SURFACE THEORY FOR THRUST AUGMENTING EJECTORS. Negotiations are to be conducted with Rockwell International, Columbus Aircraft Division, 4300 East Fifth Avenue, Columbus, OH 43216. Unsolicited proposal. See Note 46.

★ A -- DESIGN AND TEST OF LIFT FAN DESIGN for a new air cushion vehicle amphibious assault landing craft. Negotiations conducted with Bell Aerospace Textron, Division of Textron, Inc., P.O. Box 29307, New Orleans, LA 70189. See Note 46. (165)

Office of Naval Research, 800 N. Quincy St., Arlington, VA 22217.

★ A -- TURBINE ENGINE RESEARCH in the area of Turbine Engine Combustion, lean blowoff, flame radiation, smoke analysis and ignition. RFQ DAAK30-78-00128 to be negotiated with Purdue Research Foundation, West Lafayette, Indiana. Closing date 30 Jun 78. See Note 46. (166)

U.S. Army Tank Automotive Materiel Readiness Command, Warren, MI 48090

A -- CONDUCT FIRE TEST OF FLOOR FRAMED WITH COM-PLY JOISTS to determine fire resistance. Test to be conducted during last two weeks in July and completed, with written report, by August 31, 1978. RFQ SE-128(C) to be submitted by June 26, 1978. (166)

Southeastern Forest Experiment Station, P.O. Box 2570, Asheville, N C 28802 Attn: C. Swafford.

A -- DEVELOPMENT OF A SMALL, RUGGEDIZED, HAND-HELD MICROFORM VIEWER (HHMV) suitable for field combat use—RFP DAAG39-78-R-9194. Negotiations will be conducted with Washington Scientific Industries, Inc., Long Lake, Minnesota. RFP DAAG39-78-R-9194.

A -- DEVELOPMENT OF A SMALL, RUGGEDIZED, HAND-HELD MICROFORM VIEWER (HHMV) suitable for field combat use—RFP DAAG39-78-R-9195. Negotiations will be conducted with 3M Company, Microfilm Products Division, St. Paul, Minnesota.

A -- DEVELOPMENT OF A SMALL, RUGGEDIZED, HAND-HELD MICROFORM VIEWER (HHMV) suitable for field combat use—RFP DAAG39-78-R-9196. Negotiations will be conducted with Realist, Inc., Menomonee Falls, Wisconsin.

A -- ANALYSIS IN TACTICAL INTELLIGENCE APPLICATION EXPERIMENTATION/VALIDATION''—RFP DAAG39-78-R-9203. Intends to enter into negotiations with the IBM Corporation, Gaithersburg, MD

A -- COMPUTER CALCULATIONS—induced currents and fields in Army tactical shelters—RFP DAAG39-78-R-9201. Intend to negotiate with Science Applications, Inc.

A -- ARMY STUDY ENTITLED ''TECHNOLOGICAL AND SYSTEMS FORECAST FOR THE BATTLEFIELD OF 1990 - 2000''—RFP DAAG39-78-R-9202. Negotiations conducted with Forecasting International, Ltd., Arlington, VA. (165)

Contract Branch, Harry Diamond Laboratories, Adelphi, MD 20783, Attn: DELHD-CSA

A -- PROCURE AND EVALUATE ONE 18'' FOCAL LENGTH LENS cone for the KA-69A Camera in support of the P-3 photographic efforts. A contract is being negotiated exclusively with DynaMetrics, Inc., Pasadena, Calif. 91103.

A -- FABRICATION OF AN ENGINEERING MODEL of an Interactive Control Panel for the AN/AQA-7(V)4+5. A contract is being negotiated exclusively with Magnavox Company, Government and Industrial Electronics, Ft. Wayne, Indiana 46808. See Note 46.

★ A -- FEASIBILITY STUDY TO DETERMINE THE SENSITIVITY OF THEIR FREQUENCY DOMAIN ADAPTIVE LINE ENHANCEMENT ALGORITHM for different resolutions. A contract is being negotiated exclusively with Rockwell International, Autonetics Group, Anaheim, Calif. 92803. See Note 46.

★ A -- INSPECTION, ALIGNMENT, REPAIR, CALIBRATION, AND PREVENTATIVE MAINTENANCE FOR ANTENNA RANGE EQUIPMENT manufactured by Scientific Atlanta. A contract is being negotiated exclusively with Scientific Atlanta, Crofton, MD 21114. See Note 46. (165)

Naval Air Development Center, Warminster, PA 18974

★ A -- RESEARCH ON LASER GYRO ERROR AND PERFORMANCE MODELING. Unsolicited proposal. Negotiations are to be conducted with Charles Stark Draper Laboratory, Inc., 555 Technology Square, Cambridge, MA 02139. See Note 46.

★ A -- FURTHER RESEARCH CONCERNING THE ANALYTICAL INVESTIGATION OF MULTINOZZLE PLUME FLOW FIELDS. Negotiations are to be conducted with Grumman Aerospace Corporation, Research Department, Bethpage,, New York 11714. See Note 46.

★ A -- FURTHER RESEARCH CONCERNING THE EXPERIMENTAL AND ANALYTICAL STUDY OF EROSIVE BURNING OF SOLID PROPELLANTS. Negotiations are to be conducted with Atlantic Research Corporation, Research and Technology Division, Alexandria, Virginia 22003. See note 46.

Directorate of Procurement, Air Force Office of Scientific Research, Bolling AFB DC 20332

★ A -- ''SPECIAL COMMUNICATIONS''—Three months effort—Negotiations are contemplated with SRI International for R and D effort—See notes 27 and 46. (165)

U.S. Army Missile R&D Command, Attn: DRDMI-ICBB/Hollingsworth, Redstone Arsenal, AL 35809.

Content

cpf

Let's Make a Deal: Foundation Funding

It's difficult to generalize about the 25,000 foundations in the United States. They differ in size, structure, operating procedures and even fiscal years. The one universal feature of foundations, however, is that they are institutions created by the wealthy. So, foundation grants often reflect the values and perceptions of the people that control them.

The list of complaints about the way philanthropic institutions (including foundations) operate is long; the following is a summary of interviews with grantees appearing in *Philanthropy and the Powerless,* a paper prepared for the Commission on Private Philanthropy and Public Needs. Author Sarah Carey notes that the following comments "apply to some donors at some times," but that "foundations, corporations, churches and other donors are highly varied, and it is a great mistake to treat any one category as monolithic."

- *"They (philanthropic institutions) have become permanent bureaucracies with high overhead whose well-paid staffs attempt to impose their ideas of what the problems are and how they should be solved on the grantee;*

- *their approach is intellectual and overly academic, lacking an understanding of how real change is made;*

- *they have the intellectual's discomfort with the complicated machinery of democracy and particularly with the legislative and political processes (as one grantee put it, they have about as much faith in democracy as Richard Nixon had);*

- *they are faddist and won't stick with the tough, ongoing issues that plague the society;*

- *they measure progress and success by newspaper stories, sometimes creating issues through grantees that manipulate the press and believing them solved simply because they have become the subject of public debate;*

- *they spend all their time talking to each other and are unwilling to or incapable of reaching out to varied groups in the society, thereby denying access to their benefits to activitists, community groups, and others (one grantee said that there is an old-boy network of donors and donees; if you get in with one member of the foundation club, you suddenly have access to all 17 of those who entertain grants from the powerless);*

- *they are not open and forthright in informing the public about their programs, eligibility for grants, and expected performance levels;*

- *they are unwilling to stick with grantees or would-be grantees to provide them technical assistance in developing their programs, the same way they would for a university or medical institution;*

- *they impose structural requirements on grantees such as a 501 (C)(3) organization or a big name board of directors that must include a Republican one year and a union leader the next;*

- *philanthropic donors refuse to give funds to groups that lobby or engage in public activity."[1]*

Other comments that are frequently made by fund-raisers are:

- *the powerless are virtually excluded from the foundations' decision-making process; minorities, clerical workers, welfare mothers, factory workers, etc. do not appear among the ranks of foundation trustees;*

- *some foundations inquire about grantees' affirmative action plans while their own staffs and boards remain mostly white and male.*

It's worth noting that some foundations have undergone changes in recent years. More are publishing annual reports and application guidelines. Community people are the decision-makers for a handful of foundations. And some foundations are holding community discussion conferences (a chance for grantors and grantees to engage in some dialogue apart from the grant-making process). The Council on Founda-

---

[1]Carey, Sarah C., "Philanthropy and the Powerless," **Research Papers** sponsored by The Commission on Private Philanthropy and Public Needs, Volume II, Part II, Department of the Treasury, 1977. p. 1111.

tions regularly encourages its foundation members to make some modest changes while the National Committee for Responsive Philanthropy and the Grantsmanship Center have become the grantees' advocates for more substantial changes in the way foundations operate. In short, foundations are far from perfect, and grantees should be adding their perspective to the dialogue about how to make philanthropic institutions more democratic.

The Types of Foundations

There are five different varieties of foundations which have very different characteristics, primarily due to their structure.

1. **General Purpose Foundations:**

   These are the ones that have probably shaped your image of the foundation world—Ford, Rockefeller, Mellon and so on. The 400 general purpose foundations have broad goals and few geographic restrictions.

   One of the myths about foundations is that there are lots of them with lots of money. In fact, a small number (1.6% of all foundations) control 65% of all foundation assets. So when people talk about how large foundation grants are, they are undoubtedly referring to those made by general purpose foundations. Many of these foundations re-examine their funding priorities every few years, publish annual reports and employ staff people to handle the large numbers of grant requests.

2. **Family Foundations:**

   These are foundations that have been set up by wealthy individuals or families, like the Edward Austin Trust in Massachusetts which makes grants to "needy aged men and women who had been in better circumstances in early life, but had become in want in old age." Most of these 20,000 foundations (with 15% of total foundation assets) have geographic limitations, fund programs of interest to the "founding family," and tend to be less experimental and more informal in their grant-making. A very few have published annual reports; for most, applicants must rely on the 990 tax return forms to determine their funding priorities.

3. Special Purpose Foundations:

The purpose of these foundations is limited to a particular subject area, such as the Christopher Smithers Foundation in New York that concentrates on alcoholism. They number approximately 600 and control 10% of total foundation assets.

4. Corporate Foundations:

Corporate foundations restrict their giving to areas where the corporation and its branches, plants or subsidiaries are located. The 1,500 US corporate foundations are required to file 990 tax returns (unlike corporations that have not established foundations), so applicants are able to determine what the foundation has funded in the past. Applicants can check the **Foundation Center National Data Bank**, Volume I to see if corporations in their area have set up foundations.

5. Community Foundations:

The 250 community foundations are technically "public charities" because their assets are derived from multiple sources, rather than one family. With 4% of total foundation assets and total annual grants of about $60 million, community foundations fund diverse programs *in their community* and are usually more visable and experimental than family foundations. Many of them are also willing to provide technical assistance as well as grants to community groups.

Here's an example of the foundation world in one state, Massachusetts. Contrary to popular opinion, Massachusetts foundations are numerous but small; most are family foundations.

MASSACHUSETTS FOUNDATIONS

	Assets	Grants
106 foundations with assets over $1 million	$572,816,000	$24,419,000
1,325 foundations with assets under $1 million	$155,954,000	$18,209,000

Seven percent of Massachusetts foundations account for more than 50 percent of total foundation grants in the state. This means that most fundraisers concentrate their efforts on the top 100 or so foundations. The density of hospitals, colleges and other nonprofit groups in Massachusetts is such that competition for foundation money is intense.

Another factor is that most of the foundations are located in Boston, in the eastern part of the state. Citizen groups in the rural western part of the state are quick to point out that very few foundation people are aware of problems there.

The situation in Massachusetts is not unlike that in other states. The following chart contains information on foundations with assets of $1 million or more.

Assets, Gifts Received, and Grants For Foundations With Over $1 Million In Assets,a By Region and State

Place	Number	Assets (in thousands)	Gifts Received b (in thousands)	Grants c (in thousands)
New England	182	$1,072,459	$65,914	$47,593
Maine	2	4,246	-	144
New Hampshire	8	16,109	39	533
Vermont	2	9,319	451	44
Massachusetts	106	572,816	4,376	24,419
Rhode Island	10	34,095	2,298	2,232
Connecticut	54	435,874	58,750	20,221
Middle Atlantic	780	14,957,317	538,400	749,593
New York	548	10,966,185	152,060	621,152
New Jersey	59	1,609,512	315,408	39,281
Pennsylvania	173	2,381,620	70,932	89,160
East North Central	502	5,513,619	147,305	263,350
Ohio	161	984,023	33,510	61,655
Indiana	37	1,167,373	17,181	26,929
Illinois	157	818,276	28,100	61,600
Michigan	90	2,278,872	55,741	93,261
Wisconsin	57	265,075	12,773	19,905
West North Central	160	1,296,181	43,423	68,054
Minnesota	68	704,761	15,682	30,906
Iowa	17	54,331	980	5,633
Missouri	59	469,156	21,602	28,107
North Dakota	-	-	-	-
South Dakota	1	1,163	2	17
Nebraska	10	49,257	1,701	2,745
Kansas	5	17,513	3,456	646
South Atlantic	255	2,450,301	50,050	184,466
Delaware	28	230,410	2,038	74,830
Maryland	24	97,099	5,032	5,114
D.C.	29	170,945	7,284	7,907
Virginia	24	81,870	2,040	2,989
West Virginia	1	1,507	-	11
North Carolina	46	784,687	7,863	38,011
South Carolina	12	81,526	5,160	3,094
Georgia	57	847,925	8,726	46,130
Florida	34	154,332	11,907	6,480
East South Central	44	250,379	3,235	14,515
Kentucky	9	94,638	855	2,492
Tennessee	21	112,957	1,810	10,228
Alabama	13	40,024	570	1,767
Mississippi	1	2,760	-	28
West South Central	197	1,759,603	50,031	97,530
Arkansas	4	8,560	490	443
Louisiana	20	74,506	1,175	2,759
Oklahoma	26	266,787	4,330	10,462
Texas	147	1,409,750	44,036	83,866
Mountain	42	351,426	3,966	14,454
Montana	1	2,682	-	487
Idaho	4	5,171	13	624
Wyoming	2	5,611	86	358
Colorado	20	200,948	131	7,945
New Mexico	3	10,834	3,535	121
Arizona	5	15,447	9	217
Utah	6	7,621	192	407
Nevada	1	103,112	-	4,295
Pacific	218	1,302,783	75,406	70,058
Washington	27	84,587	9,578	6,275
Oregon	14	61,143	331	1,916
California	165	1,077,208	64,770	59,084
Hawaii	12	79,845	727	2,783
Outlying Areas				
Puerto Rico	1	8,490	1,529	25
Totals	2,381	$28,962,558	$979,259	$1,509,638

Source: The Foundation Center

a. Information shown for 2,381 foundations that either had assets of $1 million or more in fiscal year 1971 or early fiscal year 1972 or made grants of $500,000 or more in this period. Includes data on 48 community foundations with assets of $780 million, gifts received totalling $82.5 million, and grants totalling $38.5 million.

b. Gifts were reported for 2,078 foundations.

c. Grants-paid data lacking for 58 foundations.

Researching Foundations

Finding your way through the maze of foundation information requires persistence, patience and good eyesight (because much of the information is on microfilm). At first glance, the research process is mind-boggling, but with a little practice it becomes less mystifying.

The following questions should form the basis of the information gathering:

- *Has the foundation funded projects similar to your own (e.g. day care, youth programs, work-place organizing, etc.)?*

- *What type of funds does the foundation give (operating, unrestricted, special projects, equipment purchases, building funds, start-up or seed money)?*

- *Has the foundation funded projects in your geographic area?*

- *Is the size of grants made by the foundation appropriate to the needs of your organization?*

  (Only the largest foundations will consider underwriting the costs of an entire project, so the assumption is that project costs will be met by a number of different sources. But many of the smaller family foundations' grants range from $5 to $50. You need to decide if it's worth the time, cost and energy to submit proposals given a foundation's usual grant range.)

A good starting point is to identify foundations in or near your community. These foundations are more apt to be familiar with the problems and needs of your community.

Identifying Local Foundations

Because so much of the information about foundations deals with the "big guys," very few of the books on foundations are helpful in picking out foundations at the local level. Here are a few useful publications:

The Foundation Directory, Edition 6 ($35)
Dept. FC
Columbia University Press
136 South Broadway
Irvington, NY 10533

The latest edition lists factual information on the largest 2,818 foundations in the U.S. The Directory is best used either as a quick reference for a foundation's address, telephone number, names of trustees, or to pick out the largest foundations in a particular state. These descriptions of the foundations are usually too vague to be very helpful, so users should always refer to an annual report for the foundation or the 990 tax return form.

Example:

895
Blake (S. P.) Foundation
c/o Friendly Ice Cream Corporation
1855 Boston Road
Wilbraham 01095   (413) 543-2400

Established in 1972 in Massachusetts.

Donor(s): S. Prestley Blake.

Purpose and Activities: Educational purposes; giving limited to Massachusetts and Connecticut. No grants to individuals.

Financial Data (yr. ended 12/31/75): Assets, $1,266,078 (M); expenditures, $48,085, including $47,235 for 26 grants (high: $31,000; low: $10).

Trustees: Benson Blake, S. Prestley Blake.

Write: S. Prestley Blake, Trustee.

Grant Application Information: Initial approach by letter; submit 1 copy of proposal; no application deadline.

IRS Employer Identification No.: 237185871

The Foundation Center National Data Book

2 volumes ($40)
The Foundation Center
888 Seventh Avenue
New York, NY 10019

Volume I is an alphabetical listing of all US foundations, useful in determining the state in which a particular foundation is located and in identifying corporate foundations. In Volume II, foundations are arranged by state and then ranked according to the amount of grants paid during one year. Because the address of each foundation is included, you can easily compile a list of the foundations in your area, ranked by size.

State Foundation Directories

These state directories concentrate on foundations within a particular state and include the smaller foundations usually omitted from other directories. A listing of state foundation directories appears in the **Grantsmanship Center News,** Issue 22, October-December 1977. In Massachusetts, there are current-

ly four such directories; the best is the **Directory of Foundations in Massachusetts,** prepared by the Attorney General's Office, Division of Public Charities. A sample entry:

CRAPO (HENRY H.) CHARITABLE FOUNDATION
P.O. Box B 962, New Bedford, 02741
Officers: John C. Bullard, President; David C. Howes, Treasurer & Clerk; Roger E. Titus, Vice-President; W. Julia Underwood, Director; Karl P. Goodwin, Director.
Finances: Year ending 12/75: Assets — $613,125; Total expenditures — $48,104; Total grants — $46,000; Largest grant — $21,000; Smallest grant — $500; No. -- 8.
Interests: A. 1,2,5; B. 1,5; D. 1.
Purpose: Restricted to charities in New Bedford and surrounding communities.

Determining Funding Priorities of Local Foundations

Once you have a list of foundations in your area, the next step is to figure out the kinds of projects they've funded in the past. The brief descriptions found in most directories aren't terribly enlightening and occasionally these descriptions differ markedly from what the foundation actually funds.

The Foundation Grants Index ($20)

Prepared by The Foundation Center
Dept. FC
Columbia University Press
136 South Broadway
Irvington, NY 10533

The **Grants Index** is a cumulative listing of grants included in the previous year's issues of **Foundation News.** Three indices — key word index, index of recipients and subject category index — make the **Grants Index** a good place to begin a search for foundation funding. The information in the **Grants Index** and the **Foundation News** is by no means all-inclusive; very few foundations regularly report their grants to The Foundation Center.

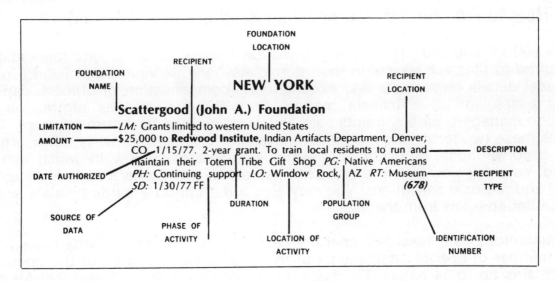

FOUNDATION
LOCATION

RECIPIENT

FOUNDATION
NAME

RECIPIENT
LOCATION

NEW YORK

Scattergood (John A.) Foundation

LIMITATION — *LM:* Grants limited to western United States

AMOUNT — $25,000 to **Redwood Institute**, Indian Artifacts Department, Denver, CO 1/15/77. 2-year grant. To train local residents to run and maintain their Totem Tribe Gift Shop *PG:* Native Americans *PH:* Continuing support *LO:* Window Rock, AZ *RT:* Museum **(678)**

DATE AUTHORIZED

SD: 1/30/77 FF

DESCRIPTION

RECIPIENT
TYPE

SOURCE OF
DATA

DURATION

POPULATION
GROUP

PHASE OF
ACTIVITY

LOCATION OF
ACTIVITY

IDENTIFICATION
NUMBER

Foundation News ($20/year)

Box 783
Old Chelsea Station
New York, NY 10011

Every two months, the **Foundation News** is published with an insert listing recent grants made by foundations who voluntarily submit their information to The Foundation Center. The entries in the News are similar to those in the **Grants Index** (see above). Either recent issues of the **Foundation News** or the latest edition of the **Grants Index** are good starting points.

Foundation Annual Reports (free)

Approximately 300 foundations in the country publish annual reports describing their past grants, funding priorities and historical information about the foundation. Annual reports surpass other resources because they are more comprehensive and current. Foundations that publish annual reports are asterisked in the **Foundation Center National Data Book**. Annual reports may be used at The Foundation Center and regional foundation collections or may be ordered directly from the individual foundations.

Foundation Center Source Book ($150)

The Foundation Center
888 Seventh Avenue
New York, NY 10019

Covering more than 500 foundations, each profile includes addresses, telephone numbers, officers,

program staff, financial data, background information, representative grants and application procedures. A good buy at 30¢ per profile, but the total cost is prohibitive for many citizen groups. Like other Foundation Center publications, this is available for use at the Center or its regional foundation collections.

990 Tax Returns

For most small foundations, this is the only place where applicants can find a list of grants made by the foundation and a telephone number. All private foundations must file annual tax returns with the Internal Revenue Service. The returns are microfilmed by IRS and aperture cards are sent to The Foundation Center and regional collections.

THE FOUNDATION CENTER

How to Find the Information You Need on an Aperture Card

Forms 990-PF and 990-AR are the information returns which private foundations are required to file each year with the Internal Revenue Service. Form 990-PF provides fiscal details on receipts and expenditures, compensation of officers, capital gains or losses, and other financial matters. Form 990-AR provides information on foundation managers, assets, grants paid and/or committed for future payment. The IRS films these two forms and makes them available on aperture cards. An aperture card is a conventional tabulator card which contains a window in which film is mounted. You may view aperture cards at The Foundation Center's main libraries or national and regional collections. You may also order aperture cards by state or on individual foundations from the IRS.

Each foundation has at least two aperture cards. Many have more cards depending on the number of special attachments to the return. The film part of the aperture card contains up to 14 pages. The basic pages of Forms 990-PF and 990-AR are always filmed in the same sequence and will be found in the same location on each card. The 990-PF and 990-AR are each filmed on a separate card from left to right in three consecutive rows.

Below is a reproduction of the aperture cards containing the forms 990-AR (upper) and 990-PF (lower).

990-AR

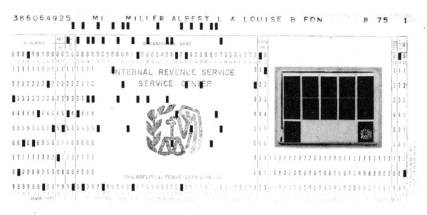

990-PF

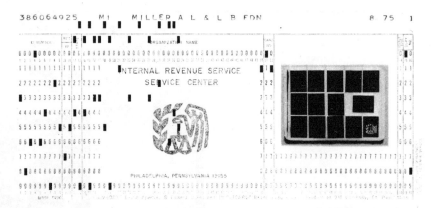

Where You'll Find Important Information on IRS Forms 990-PF and 990-AR

The following items of information on Forms 990-PF and 990-AR are those which are most commonly sought by fund seekers. The number preceding each item below also appears within a circle on the facsimiles of selected pages from the forms to show its location.

1. **Name and address of the foundation** (990-PF, p. 1 and 990-AR, p. 2).

2. **Assets at market value** (990-PF, p. 1). If this space is blank or if you wish more detailed information on the nature of the foundation's assets, see p. 3 of Form 990-AR.

3. **Telephone number** (990-PF, p. 1). This may not be the number of the foundation but instead that of an accountant or other fiscal agent, such as a bank, that maintains the books of the foundation. Therefore you may not be able to obtain by phone the information you are seeking.

4. **Gross contributions, gifts, grants, etc. (received)** (990-PF, p. 1, line 1). If the foundation received any gifts during the year, a detailed listing of all grants of $5,000 or more must be supplied on a separate schedule. (For definition of a schedule, see below.) The schedule includes: name of the donor, address, and amount contributed to the foundation. Names of donors in earlier years may appear on p. 2 of Form 990-AR.

5. **Contributions, gifts, grants (paid)** (990-PF, p. 1, line 23). If the number of grants is small, the list may appear on p. 4 of Form 990-AR. Frequently, however, you'll find the note, "see attached schedule." The IRS does not require a foundation to state its purposes, but you may be able to draw your own conclusions about its purposes by examining the list of grants.

6. **Principal foundation officer** (990-AR, top of p. 2).

7. **Officers and trustees or directors (foundation managers)** (990-AR, p. 2). Sometimes you'll find the note, "see attached schedule."

Schedule: a separate sheet of paper containing information which is required but for which there is no space or inadequate space on the form itself. Schedules are not filmed in any fixed sequence. When necessary, they are continued on subsequent cards.

990-PF

Form **990-PF**
Department of the Treasury
Internal Revenue Service

Return of Private Foundation Exempt from Income Tax
Under Section 501(c)(3) of the Internal Revenue Code

1974

For the calendar year 1974, or taxable year beginning .... 1974 and ending .... , 19 ....

Please type, print or attach label. See Instruction I.

Name of organization	Employer identification number (see instruction I)
Address (number and street) ①	Date of exemption letter
City or town, State and ZIP code	Fair market value of assets at end of year (see instruction S) ②

Enter the name and address used on your return for 1973 (if the same as above, write "Same"). If none filed, give reason.

Foreign organizations check here ▶
If exemption application is pending, check here ▶
Date created (see instruction T)

The books are in care of ▶ ....
Located at ▶ .... Telephone No. .... ③
Enter your principal activity codes from last page of instructions .... , ... , ▶ ....

Part I Analysis of Receipts and Expenditures (See instructions for Part I)	(A) Receipts and expenditures per books	(B) Computation of Net Investment Income	(C) Computation of Adjusted Net Income	(D) Disbursements for Exempt Purpose
④ 1 Gross contributions, gifts, grants, etc. (see instructions)				
2 Contributions from split-interest trusts (see instructions)				
3 Gross dues and assessments				
4 Interest				
5 Dividends				
6 Gross rents and royalties				
7 Net gain or (loss) from sale of assets not in line 11				
8 Net capital gain (see instructions)				
9 Net short-term capital gain (see instructions)				
10 Income modifications (see instructions)				
11 Gross profit from any business activities: (Gross receipts $........ less cost of sales $........ see instructions)				
12 Other income (attach schedule)				
13 Total—add lines 1 through 12				
14 Compensation of officers, etc. (see instructions)				
15 Other salaries and wages				
16 (a) Pension plan contributions				
(b) Other employee benefits				
17 Investment, legal and other professional services				
18 Interest				
19 Taxes (see instructions)				
20 Depreciation, amortization, and depletion (see instructions)				
21 Rent				
22 Other expenses (attach schedule)				
⑤ 23 Contributions, gifts, grants (see instructions)				
24 Total—add lines 14 through 23				
25 Line 13 less line 24: (a) Excess of receipts over expenditures				
(b) Net investment income				
(c) Adjusted net income (see instructions)				

Part II Excise Tax On Investment Income

1 Domestic organizations—enter 4% of line 25(b), Part I
2 Foreign organizations—(a) enter total of lines 4, 5, and 6, col. B, Part I
(b) enter 4% of line 2(a)
3 Credits: (a) Foreign organizations—tax withheld at source
(b) tax paid with application for extension of time to file (Form 2758)
4 Tax Due—line 1 or line 2(b) less line 3 . Pay in full with return. Make check or money order payable to Internal Revenue Service ▶ (Write Employer Identification Number on check or money order)
5 Overpayment—line 3 less line 1 or line 2
Foreign organization—Enter book value $ .... and fair market value $ .... of investment assets held

Under penalties of perjury, I declare that I have examined this return, including accompanying schedules and statements, and to the best of my knowledge and belief it is true, correct, and complete. If prepared by a person other than taxpayer, his declaration is based on all information of which he has any knowledge.

| Date | Signature of officer or trustee | Title |
| Date | Signature and Emp. Ident. or Soc. Sec. No. of preparer | Address of preparer |

990-AR

Form **990 — AR (1974)**   Page **2**

Annual report for calendar year 1974, or fiscal year beginning .... , 1974, and ending .... , 19 ....

Name of organization	Employer identification number
Address of principal office ①	
If books and records are not at above address, specify where they are kept	Name of principal officer of foundation ⑥

Public Inspection (See Instruction C):
(a) Enter date the notice of availability of annual report appeared in newspaper ....
(b) Enter name of newspaper ....
(c) Check ☐ if you have attached a copy of the newspaper notice as required by instruction "C." (If the notice is not attached, the report will be considered incomplete.)

Revenues

1 Amount of gifts, grants, bequests, and contributions received for the year
2 Gross income for the year
3   Total

Disbursements and Expenses

4 Disbursements for the year for the purposes for which exempt (including administrative expenses)
5 Expenses attributable to gross income (item 2 above) for the year

Foundation Managers

6 List all managers of the foundation (see section 4946(b) IRC):

Name and title	Address where manager may be contacted during normal business hours
⑦	

6a List here any managers of the foundation (see section 4946(b) IRC) who have contributed 2 percent of the total contributions received by the foundation before the close of any taxable year (but only if they have contributed more than $5,000). (See section 507(d)(2).) ④

6b List here any managers of the foundation (see section 4946(b) IRC) who own 10 percent or more of the stock of a corporation (or an equally large portion of the ownership of a partnership or other entity) of which the foundation has a 10 percent or greater interest.

990-AR

Form 990 – AR (1974)   Page 3

Balance Sheet Per Books at the Beginning of the Year

Assets		Liabilities	
Cash		Accounts payable	
Accounts and notes receivable		Contributions, gifts, grants, etc. payable	
Inventories		Bonds and notes payable	
Securities		Mortgages payable	
Government obligations		Other liabilities	
Corporate bonds		Total liabilities	
Corporate stocks		**Net Worth**	
Mortgage loans		Principal fund	
Real estate			
Less Depreciation		Income fund	
Other assets			
Less Depreciation		Total net worth	
Total assets		Total liabilities and net worth	

Itemized Statement of Securities and All Other Assets Held at the Close of the Taxable Year

Asset	Book value	Market value
②		
Total		

990-AR

Form 990 – AR (1974)   Page 4

Grants and Contributions Paid or Approved for Future Payment During the Year

Recipient — Name and address (home or business)	If recipient is an individual, show any relationship to any foundation manager or substantial contributor	Concise statement of purpose of grant or contribution	Amount
Paid during year ⑤			
Total			
Approved for future payment			
Total			

A notice has been published that this Annual Report is available for public inspection at the principal office of the foundation, and copies of this Annual Report have been furnished to the Attorney of each State entitled to receive reports as required by instruction "F."

Date	Signature of foundation manager	Title
Date	Signature of individual or firm preparing the report	Preparer's address Emp. Ident. or Soc. Sec. No.

Instructions

A. Annual Report.—An annual report is required from the foundation managers (as defined in section 4946(b)) of every organization which is a private foundation, including a trust described in section 4947(a)(1) which is treated as a private foundation, having at least $5,000 of assets at any time during a taxable year. A private foundation may use this form for its annual reporting requirements.

If you prefer not to use this form, you may prepare the report in printed, typewritten or any other form you choose, provided it readily and legibly discloses the information required by section 6056 and the regulations thereunder.

The annual report is in addition to and not in lieu of submitting the information required on Form 990-PF under section 6033.

B. Where and When to File.—The annual report must be filed at the time and place specified for filing Form 990-PF.

C. Public Inspection of Private Foundation's Annual Reports.—As a foundation manager, you must make the annual report required by section 6056 available at the principal office of the foundation for inspection during regular business hours by any citizen who so requests within 180 days after publication of notice of its availability; or, if you choose, you may furnish a copy free of charge to such persons requesting inspection, provided these persons do so at the time and manner prescribed in section 6104(d) and the regulations thereunder.

The notice must be published not later than the day prescribed for filing the annual report (determined with regard to any extensions of time for filing), in a newspaper having general circulation in the county in which the principal office of the private foundation is located. The notice must state that the annual report of the private foundation is available at its principal office during regular business hours for inspection by any citizen who so requests within 180 days after the date of the publication. It must also show the address of the private foundation's principal office and the name of its principal manager. A private foundation may designate in addition to its principal office, or none other than the residence of a substantial contributor or foundation manager) instead of such office, any other location where its annual report is available.

The term "newspaper having general circulation" shall include any newspaper or journal which is permitted to publish statements in satisfaction of State statutory requirements relating to transfer of title to real estate or other similar legal notices.

A copy of the notice must be attached to the annual report filed with the Internal Revenue Service.

A private foundation which has terminated its status as such under section 507(b)(1)(A), by distributing all its net assets to one or more public charities without retaining any right, title or interest in such assets, does not have to publish notice of availability of its annual report or furnish such report to the public for the taxable year in which it so terminates (Reg. 1.507-2(a)(6)).

D. Signature and Verification.—The report must be signed by the foundation manager.

E. List of States.—A private foundation is required to attach to its Form 990-PF a list of all States:

(a) to which the organization reports in any fashion concerning its organization, assets, or activities; and

(b) with which the organization has registered (or which it has otherwise notified in any manner) that it intends to be, or is a charitable organization or that it is, or intends to be, a holder of property devoted to a charitable purpose.

F. Furnishing of Copies to State Officers; Listing of States.—The foundation managers must furnish a copy of the annual report (required by section 6056) to the Attorney General of (1) each State listed for Form 990-PF above, (2) the State in which the principal office of the foundation is located, and (3) the State in which the foundation was incorporated or organized. Such report must be furnished at the same time it is sent to the Internal Revenue Service. In addition, the foundation managers shall provide upon request a copy of the annual report to the Attorney General or other appropriate State officer of any other State. The foundation manager shall also attach to the report a copy of the Form 990-PF (or Schedule PF (Form 1041) for a 4947(a)(1) trust) and a copy of the Form 4720 (if any) filed by the foundation with the Internal Revenue Service for the year.

G. Penalty for Failure to File Report and Notice on Time.—If a private foundation fails to file the annual report on or before the due date, or to comply with the requirements under "C" above, there will be imposed on the person (anyone under a duty to perform the act), a $10 penalty for each day during which the failure continues, not to exceed $5,000. (See section 6652(d)(3).) If more than one person is liable, all such persons shall be jointly and severally liable with respect to such failure. Organizations that have given notice under section 508(b) as to their status and have not received a letter from the Internal Revenue Service containing a determination as to such status—refer to Revenue Procedure 72-31, 1972-1 C.B. 759, or later revisions, for rules relating to relief from the penalty provision of Section 6652. If the failure to file the annual report or comply with "C" is willful, there will be imposed, in addition to the amount mentioned above, a penalty of $1,000 for each such report or notice. (See section 6685.)

H. Foreign Organizations.—A foreign organization which has received substantially all of its support (other than gross investment income) from sources outside the United States will not be subject to the requirements of instructions "C" and "F" above.

The Foundation Center
888 Seventh Avenue
New York, New York 10019

THE FOUNDATION CENTER

The Foundation Center makes available factual information on philanthropic foundations through programs of library service, publication, and research. Foundation Center libraries contain all of the Center's standard reference works, recent books and reports on foundations, foundation annual reports on microfiche, and information returns filed by foundations with the Internal Revenue Service. Each collection contains the IRS returns for most foundations located within its state, while several, as indicated below, also cover foundations in adjacent states. A complete set covering all U.S. foundations can be found at the national libraries. Users should telephone individual libraries for a current schedule of hours.

Where to Go for Information on Foundation Funding

Foundation Center National Libraries

The Foundation Center
888 Seventh Avenue
New York, New York 10019

The Foundation Center
1001 Connecticut Avenue, N.W.
Washington, D.C. 20036

Foundation Center Field Offices

The Foundation Center — San Francisco
312 Sutter Street
San Francisco, California 94108

The Foundation Center — Cleveland
Kent H. Smith Library
739 National City Bank Building
629 Euclid Avenue
Cleveland, Ohio 44114

National Cooperating Collection

Donors Forum of Chicago
208 South LaSalle Street
Chicago, Illinois 60604

Regional Cooperating Collections

ALABAMA
Birmingham Public Library
2020 Seventh Avenue, North
Birmingham 35203

Auburn University at Montgomery
Library
Montgomery 36117

ALASKA
University of Alaska, Anchorage
Library
3211 Providence Drive
Anchorage 99504

ARIZONA
Tuscon Public Library
Main Library
200 S. Sixth Avenue
Tuscon 85701

ARKANSAS
Little Rock Public Library
Reference Department
700 Louisiana Street
Little Rock 72201

CALIFORNIA
University Research Library
Reference Department
University of California
Los Angeles 90024

San Diego Public Library
820 E Street
San Diego 92101

COLORADO
Denver Public Library
Sociology Division
1357 Broadway
Denver 80203

CONNECTICUT
Hartford Public Library
Reference Department
500 Main Street
Hartford 06103

FLORIDA
Jacksonville Public Library
Business, Science, and Industry Department
122 North Ocean Street
Jacksonville 32202

Miami – Dade Public Library
Florida Collection
One Biscayne Boulevard
Miami 33132

GEORGIA
Atlanta Public Library
126 Carnegie Way, N W
Atlanta 30303
(also covers Alabama, Florida, South Carolina, and Tennessee)

HAWAII
Thomas Hale Hamilton Library
University of Hawaii
Humanities and Social Sciences Division
2550 The Mall
Honolulu 96822

IDAHO
Caldwell Public Library
1010 Dearborn Street
Caldwell 83605

ILLINOIS
Sangamon State University Library
Shepherd Road
Springfield 62708

INDIANA
Indianapolis – Marion County Public
Library
40 East St. Clair Street
Indianapolis 46204

IOWA
Des Moines Public Library
100 Locust Street
Des Moines 50309

KANSAS
Topeka Public Library
Adult Services Department
1515 West Tenth Street
Topeka 66604

KENTUCKY
Louisville Free Public Library
Fourth and York Streets
Louisville 40203

LOUISIANA
New Orleans Public Library
Business and Science Division
219 Loyola Avenue
New Orleans 70140

MAINE
University of Maine at Portland-Gorham
Center for Research and Advanced Study
246 Deering Avenue
Portland 04102

MARYLAND
Enoch Pratt Free Library
Social Science and History Department
400 Cathedral Street
Baltimore 21201
(also covers District of Columbia)

33333333333333333

MASSACHUSETTS
Associated Foundation of Greater Boston
294 Washington Street, Suite 501
Boston 02108

Boston Public Library
Copley Square
Boston 02117

MICHIGAN
Henry Ford Centennial Library
15301 Michigan Avenue
Dearborn 48126

Purdy Library
Wayne State University
Detroit 48202

Grand Rapids Public Library
Sociology and Education Department
Library Plaza
Grand Rapids 49502

MINNESOTA
Minneapolis Public Library
Sociology Department
300 Nicollet Mall
Minneapolis 55401
(also covers North and South Dakota)

MISSISSIPPI
Jackson Metropolitan Library
301 North State Street
Jackson 39201

MISSOURI
Kansas City Public Library
311 East 12th Street
Kansas City 64106
(also covers Kansas)

The Danforth Foundation Library
222 South Central Avenue
St. Louis 63105

Springfield – Greene County Library
397 East Central Street
Springfield 65801

MONTANA
Eastern Montana College Library
Reference Department
Billings 59101

NEBRASKA
W. Dale Clark Library
Social Sciences Department
215 South 15th Street
Omaha 68102

NEW HAMPSHIRE
The New Hampshire Charitable Fund
One South Street
Concord 03301

NEW JERSEY
New Jersey State Library
Reference Section
185 West State Street
Trenton 08625

NEW MEXICO
New Mexico State Library
300 Don Gaspar Street
Santa Fe 87501

NEW YORK
New York State Library
State Education Department
Education Building
Albany 12224

Buffalo and Erie County Public Library
Lafayette Square
Buffalo 14203

Levittown Public Library
Reference Department
One Bluegrass Lane
Levittown 11756

Rochester Public Library
Business and Social Sciences Division
115 South Avenue
Rochester 14604

NORTH CAROLINA
William R. Perkins Library
Duke University
Durham 27706

OKLAHOMA
Oklahoma City Community Foundation
1300 North Broadway
Oklahoma City 73103

Tulsa City-County Library System
400 Civic Center
Tulsa 74103

OREGON
Library Association of Portland
Education and Psychology Department
801 S.W. Tenth Avenue
Portland 97205

PENNSYLVANIA
The Free Library of Philadelphia
Logan Square
Philadelphia 19103
(also covers Delaware)

Hillman Library
University of Pittsburgh
Pittsburgh 15213

RHODE ISLAND
Providence Public Library
Reference Department
150 Empire Street
Providence 02903

SOUTH CAROLINA
South Carolina State Library
Reader Services Department
1500 Senate Street
Columbia 29211

TENNESSEE
Memphis Public Library
1850 Peabody Avenue
Memphis 38104

TEXAS
The Hogg Foundation for Mental Health
The University of Texas
Austin 78712

Dallas Public Library
History and Social Sciences Division
1954 Commerce Street
Dallas 75201
(also covers Arkansas, Louisiana, New Mexico, and Oklahoma)

El Paso Community Foundation
El Paso National Bank Building, Suite 1616
El Paso 79901

Minnie Stevens Piper Foundation
201 North St. Mary's Street
San Antonio 78205

UTAH
Salt Lake City Public Library
Information and Adult Services
209 East Fifth Street
Salt Lake City 84111

VERMONT
State of Vermont Department of Libraries
Reference Services Unit
111 State Street
Montpelier 05602

VIRGINIA
Richmond Public Library
Business, Science, & Technology
   Department
101 East Franklin Street
Richmond 23219

WASHINGTON
Seattle Public Library
1000 Fourth Avenue
Seattle 98104

Spokane Public Library
Reference Department
West 906 Main Avenue
Spokane 99201

WEST VIRGINIA
Kanawha County Public Library
123 Capitol Street
Charleston 25301

WISCONSIN
Marquette University Memorial Library
1415 West Wisconsin Avenue
Milwaukee 53233
(also covers Illinois)

WYOMING
Laramie County Community College
   Library
1400 East College Drive
Cheyenne 82001

PUERTO RICO
Consumer Education and Service Center
Department of Consumer Affairs
Minillas Central Government
   Building North
Santurce 00908
(covers selected foundations)

MEXICO
Biblioteca Benjamin Franklin
Londres 16
Mexico City 6, D.F.
(covers selected foundations)

3/78

Identifying Out-of-State Foundations

Your files of local foundations should now be fairly comprehensive, but you may be wondering if there are foundations outside of the region or state which might be interested in your project. Below are some questions to consider in researching national foundations.

- *Does the foundation appear to have any geographic restrictions? Has it ever funded organizations in your state or region?*

- *Does the foundation express an interest only in "demonstration or model projects," projects that can be duplicated in other regions of the country if the approach is successful?*

- *Has your organization received sufficient local support to increase its credibility in the eyes of national foundations?*

- *Unlike smaller foundations, many national foundations develop different funding priorities each year: What percentage of the foundation's funds have gone to similar projects in the last year? Does the foundation's annual report suggest new priorities for the coming year?*

Network of Change Oriented Foundations

Playboy Foundation
919 North Michigan Avenue
Chicago, IL 60611

This is a helpful directory for social change groups, but it should be supplemented with information from the foundation's annual report or 990 tax return.

The Foundation Grants Index

Either the **Grants Index, Foundation News,** or their computerized equivalent, **Comsearch Printouts**

(Foundation Center, 888 Seventh Avenue, New York, NY 10019), are useful in identifying out-of-state foundations. The **Foundation Center Source Book Profiles** described above is also helpful because it includes all the information you'll need in one place.

Foundation Reporter, Trustees of Wealth, and News Monitor of Philanthropy

Taft Corporation
1000 Vermont Avenue, Suite 600
Washington, D.C. 20005

The **Foundation Reporter** is a more expensive version of **The Foundation Center Source Book Profiles. Trustees of Wealth** gives biographical data on foundation trustees, and the **News Monitor** is similar to **Foundation News.** Purchasers cannot buy the volumes separately; they must be purchased by "systems."

System 1: **Foundation Reporter, Trustees of Wealth, New Monitor,** and **Hot Line** news service ($375)

System 2: **Foundation Reporter, News Monitor,** and **Hot Line** ($275)

System 3: **Trustees of Wealth, News Monitor,** and **Hot Line** ($125)

990 Tax Returns and Annual Reports

If the out-of-state foundations you've identified are not included in any of the above, consult the foundation's annual report or 990 tax return form.

Frequently Asked Questions

1. *IS IT ADVISABLE TO SEND LETTERS OR PROPOSALS TO ALL THE MASSACHUSETTS FOUNDATIONS IN* **THE FOUNDATION DIRECTORY** *RATHER THAN SPEND ALL THAT TIME DOING RESEARCH?*

    How do foundations react to this "shotgun approach?" According to one foundation trustee, "We look for applicants who've done their homework — who've sent us a proposal because their program matches our own funding priorities. When the word travels that many foundations have received the same proposal at the same time, it's apparent that the applicant wasn't very selective about choosing appropriate foundations."

    An additional disadvantage of mailing out tons of proposals or letters at once is the difficulty of following up each one.

    One approach is to send out five to ten proposals at a time, follow them up with telephone calls and wait until the funding decisions are made. If one or two of the foundations approve a grant and you still need more funds for the project, another batch of five to ten proposals can be sent out. In the cover letters for this second round, you might want to mention any funding commitments you've received for the project.

The Great Speckled Bird/cpf

For example, you might say, "The total cost of this project is $20,000, and to date we've received $1,000 from the ABC Fund and $2,000 from individual donations. We are requesting $2,000 from you." This gives the funding source the current status of the fund drive and it also creates a "snowball effect." Once one foundation approves a grant, others are likely to follow suit.

2. *OFTEN, THE ONLY INFORMATION ABOUT A FOUNDATION'S PRIORITIES IS THE LIST OF ORGANIZATIONS THAT HAVE RECEIVED FUNDING IN THE PAST FROM THE 990 TAX RETURN FORM. IS THERE A WAY TO DE-CIPER THIS LIST?*

    Here you sit, staring into the microfilm machine at this list of grants:

Stavros Foundation	$750
Kangaroo's Pouch	500
Dynamy, Inc.	500
Project Place	600

    It's no wonder you're puzzled. True enough, all the grant recipients and the amount of each grant are dutifully supplied by the foundation, but often without a clue about the purpose of the grant. One option is to ask the librarian of the collection if (s)he knows anything about the grant recipients in question. Or, if there are any directories of non-profit agencies lying about, consult them for a description of the organizations.

    You could also check a few issues of **Foundation News.** There's an index of grant recipients, enabling you to look up specific grants made to them. A description of the purpose of the grant and the type of organization is included. As a last resort, try calling the organizations themselves.

3. *MANY SMALL FOUNDATIONS ARE NOT LISTED IN THE TELEPHONE BOOK. WHERE CAN PHONE NUMBERS BE FOUND?*

The Foundation Directory, Edition 6, lists the phone numbers for the 2,818 foundations included in the directory. For smaller foundations, refer to their annual reports or Page 1 of their 990 tax return form. The addresses of some foundations may reveal that the foundation is administered by a law firm or bank.

4. *ONLY A FEW FOUNDATIONS PUBLISH APPLICATION DEADLINES. WHERE CAN THAT INFORMATION BE FOUND?*

Most of the foundations that publish annual reports indicate deadlines for submitting proposals or they at least mention the frequency of trustees' meetings when grants are approved. Unfortunately, the 990s do not contain that critical piece of information.

Most small foundations operate very informally, calling a meeting of the trustees when the stack of proposals starts to tip over, or they meet "at the discretion of the trustees" — which means anything from once a year to once a month.

One possibility is to contact foundations that seem like good prospects, asking them for the dates of their next trustees' meeting. Or, simply send in your proposal, follow it up with a phone call and assume that the foundation will be meeting sometime within the next year.

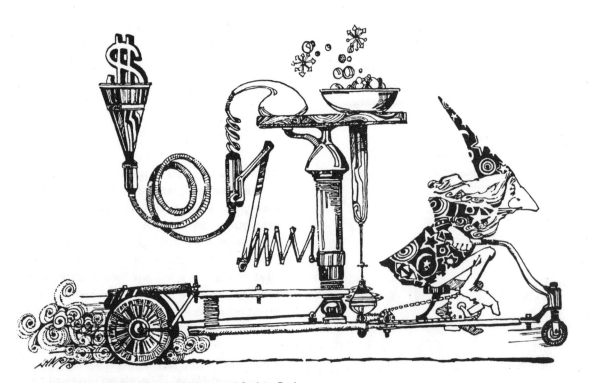

Reprinted by permission from the Business and Society Review,
Fall, 1975, No. 15, Copyright 1975 Warren, Gorham and Lamont, Inc.
210 South Street, Boston, Mass. All rights reserved.

The Corporate Connection

cpf

"Community relations at Kemper is viewed as an investment, a something-for-something proposition. Though based on a sincere interest in serving, community relations is not do-goodism; it is a profitable investment of money and time. A company that does its share as a good corporate citizen in the community can expect to be rewarded by a receptive environment in which to operate."

--(Kemper Annual Report, May 16, 1978, p. 10)

Reprinted by permission of Center for Community Economic Development.

Corporations and social change groups seldom mix well. Corporations are in business to make money; social change groups want to distribute political or economic power more equitably. If your group is working on the root causes of problems, seeking funding from most corporations may be a difficult route to take.

Likewise, any group that takes on an issue that directly threatens the way corporations operate is not likely to be a prime candidate for corporate funding. Some community groups, however, such as tutoring programs for youth, community development and manpower development programs, and summer recreational programs have received funding from corporations.

In 1976, corporate profits were estimated at $147.8 billion. Corporate grants during the same year totaled $1.35 billion, roughly 1% of pre-tax profits. The primary beneficiaries of corporate dollars have been United Way campaigns (often called the corporate stepchild), national health associations, hospitals, universities, some secondary schools and a smattering of community social service and cultural organizations.

Researching Corporations

Corporations tend to give close to home — in communities where their headquarters, plants and subsidiaries are located. For this reason, citizen groups ought to begin their search for assistance in their community.

Some questions to keep in mind while researching corporations are:

- *Is the corporation's headquarters, plant or subsidiary located in the community you're working in?*

- *Has the corporation set up a foundation to administer its corporate gifts program? (Corporations are not required to disclose grant information; foundations are.)*

- *Other than grants, in what ways could the corporation help your group?*

- *Have the corporation's profits been increasing or decreasing in recent years? (A decline in profits generally means a decline in contributions and vice versa.)*

Identifying Local Corporations

Chamber of Commerce Membership Rosters (free)

Many local Chambers of Commerce will send out lists of their members. Usually, they include only the name and addresses of local corporations, large and small.

Million Dollar Directory

Dun and Bradstreet
99 Church Street
New York, NY 10007

This hefty volume includes corporations with sales of $1 million or more. It contains a geographic index, arranged by state and town. With the names of

corporations in your community, refer to the text for more information. A sample entry:

D·U·N·S 00·695·6049
MASSACHUSETTS MUTL LIFE INSUR (MA)
1295 State St, Springfield, MA 01111
Tel (413) 788·8411　　*Sales* 1240MM　　*Emp* 4100
SIC 6311 6512
Life Insurance & Nonresidential Building Operator

•James R Martin	Ch Bd
•William J Clark	Pr
•J Berkley Ingram Jr	Ex VP
C Norman Peacor	Ex VP
A Peter Quinn Jr	Ex VP
George E Hopkins	Sr VP Gp
Edward J Kulik	Sr VP R E Investment
Richard G Dooley	VP Securities Investment
Henry H Frisbie	VP New Business
J Walter Reardon	VP Corp Comm
R Allison Johnson	VP Corp Prs
Roland P Laferriere	VP Policyholder Svce
David J Blackwell	VP Information Svcs
Walter C Wilson	VP Agency
Donald F Ryan	VP Comp
Thomas J Finnegan Jr	Sec
Edward J Lapinski	Pur
Wilson Brunel	Robert J Gaudrault
Paul Hallingby Jr	Robert H Craft
John F Watlington Jr	Philip A Singleton
Don G Mitchell	H R Bright
E Weldon Schumacher	Maurice Lazarus
Robert K Mueller	James G Harlow Jr
Robert B Atkinson	Richard N Frank
Floyd A Bond	James F Calvert
Donald F McCullough	Albert E Steiger
Bert E Phillips	

Middle Market Directory

Dun and Bradstreet
99 Church Street
New York, NY 10007

This lists smaller corporations and also has a geographic index arranged by state and town.

Register of Corporations, Directors and Executives

Standard and Poor's
345 Hudson Street
New York, NY 10014

The Register is similar to Dun and Bradstreet's materials, so use one or the other. They both are available in most public library reference departments. Sample entry:

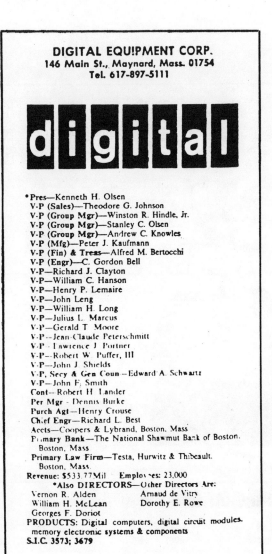

Moody's Manuals

Moody's Investor Services, Inc.
99 Church Street
New York, NY 10007

Moody's publishes several volumes by industry type, such as its **Bank and Finance Manual, Insurance Manual** and **Industrial Manual.** The information is more extensive than that found in other directories, giving you a history of the corporation, financial information, a list of directors and a lengthy list of officers. It's often easier to find the name of a contact person in the manuals, although it takes some searching and guesswork. Public relations, community affairs or civic affairs departments generally yield the most information.

132

Identifying the Most "Profitable" Corporations

In addition to the directories listed above, two business magazines publish annual listings of the largest U.S. corporations.

Double 500 Directory '78 ($6.00)

Fortune Magazine
P.O. Box 46
Trenton, NJ 08607

Fortune publishes three rankings of corporations:

- "Fortune 500," the top 500 industrial corporations

- "Second 500," the next 500 industrial corporations

  "Fifty Largest," non-industrial corporations

These are compiled into the Fortune **Double 500 Directory** and may be ordered from the address above. Sample:

When poor people take things, it's called looting. When rich people take things, it's called profits.

THE 500 LARGEST INDUSTRIAL CORPORATIONS (ranked by sales)

RANK '77	RANK '76	COMPANY	SALES ($000)	ASSETS ($000)	ASSETS RANK	NET INCOME ($000)	NET INCOME RANK
1	2	**General Motors** (Detroit)	54,961,300	26,658,300	2	3,337,500	1
2	1	**Exxon** (New York)	54,126,219*	38,453,336	1	2,422,964	3
3	3	**Ford Motor** (Dearborn, Mich.)	37,841,500	19,241,300	4	1,672,800	4
4	5	**Mobil** (New York)	32,125,828*	20,575,967	3	1,004,670	8
5	4	**Texaco** (White Plains, N.Y.)	27,920,499	18,926,026	6	930,789	9
6	6	**Standard Oil of California** (San Francisco)	20,917,331	14,822,347	7	1,016,360	6
7	8	**International Business Machines** (Armonk, N.Y.)	18,133,184	18,978,445	5	2,719,414	2
8	7	**Gulf Oil** (Pittsburgh)	17,840,000*	14,225,000	8	752,000	10
9	9	**General Electric** (Fairfield, Conn.)	17,518,600	13,696,800	9	1,088,200	5
10	10	**Chrysler** (Highland Park, Mich.)	16,708,300	7,668,200	18	163,200**	66
11	11	**International Tel. & Tel.** (New York)	13,145,664	12,285,522	11	550,667	15
12	12	**Standard Oil (Ind.)** (Chicago)	13,019,939*	12,884,286	10	1,011,575	7
13	15	**Atlantic Richfield** (Los Angeles)	10,969,091	11,119,012	12	701,515	12
14	13	**Shell Oil** (Houston)	10,112,062*	8,876,754	14	735,094	11
15	14	**U.S. Steel** (Pittsburgh)	9,609,900	9,914,400	13	137,900	84
16	16	**E. I. du Pont de Nemours** (Wilmington, Del.)	9,434,800	7,430,600	19	545,100	16
17	17	**Continental Oil** (Stamford, Conn.)	8,700,317	6,625,229	21	380,626	26
18	18	**Western Electric** (New York)	8,134,604	5,875,543	23	490,076	18
19	20	**Tenneco** (Houston)	7,440,300	8,278,300	15	426,900	21
20	19	**Procter & Gamble** (Cincinnati)[1]	7,284,255	4,487,186	31	461,463	19

Forbes ($21/year or $2.50 for the May issue)

60 Fifth Avenue
New York, NY 10011

This magazine has a similar listing, usually published in May every year. Corporations are ranked by sales, profits, assets, market value and number of employees.
Samples:

The Forbes Assets 500

U.S. companies expanded their assets last year partly because they had to, partly because they could.

Rank 1977	Rank 1976	Company	Assets ($000,000)	% Change Over 1976
1	1	American Tel & Tel	93,972	8.4
2	2	BankAmerica Corp	81,989	10.9
3	3	Citicorp	77,112	20.0
4	4	Chase Manhattan	53,180	16.5
5	5	Exxon	38,453	5.8
6	7	Mfrs Hanover Corp	35,788	13.7
7	6	Fedl Natl Mortgage	33,980	4.9
8	8	J P Morgan & Co	31,664	10.1
9	9	Chemical New York	30,706	15.4
10	10	General Motors	26,512	8.9
11	12	Continental Illinois	25,800	17.4
12	11	Bankers Trust NY	23,474	5.5
13	15	Sears, Roebuck	23,086	22.4
14	13	First Chicago Corp	22,614	14.0
15	14	Western Bancorp	22,488	14.3
16	18	Aetna Life & Cas	20,806	14.4
17	16	Mobil	20,576	9.6
18	20	Intl Tel & Tel	19,896	13.4
19	22	Ford Motor	19,224	22.1
20	19	IBM	18,978	7.1
21	17	Texaco	18,926	4.0
22	21	Security Pacific	18,736	14.2
23	27	Wells Fargo	15,359	18.4
24	26	Travelers	15,090	12.9
25	23	Standard Oil Calif	14,816	7.6
26	24	General Tel & Elec	14,687	8.0
27	25	Gulf Oil	14,225	5.8
28	28	General Electric	13,697	13.7
29	29	Standard Oil Ind	12,884	14.9
30	34	Charter New York	12,586	23.3
31	31	Crocker Natl Corp	12,450	16.2
32	33	American Express	12,346	19.2

The Forbes Profits 500

Profits of the top 500 companies improved "only" 13.3% last year, compared with a 22.6% gain the year before. But look what they were improving on top of.

Rank 1977	Rank 1976	Company	Net Profits ($000,000)	% Change Over 1976	Cash Flow ($000,000)	Rank 1977
1	1	American Tel & Tel	4,543.9	18.7	9,589	1
2	2	General Motors	3,337.5	15.0	5,718	2
3	4	IBM	2,719.4	13.4	4,525	3
4	3	Exxon	2,423.0	–8.3	3,981	4
5	5	Ford Motor	1,672.8	70.2	2,789	5
6	7	General Electric	1,088.2	16.9	1,610	9
7	9	Standard Oil Calif	1,016.4	15.5	1,597	10
8	8	Standard Oil Ind	1,011.6	13.3	1,813	6
9	6	Mobil	1,004.7	6.6	1,754	7
10	10	Texaco	930.8	7.0	1,637	8
11	13	Sears, Roebuck	836.3	21.8	1,041	16
12	11	Gulf Oil	752.0	–7.9	1,436	12
13	12	Shell Oil	735.1	4.1	1,466	11
14	16	Atlantic Richfield	701.5	22.0	1,358	14
15	14	Eastman Kodak	643.4	–1.1	982	19
16	20	General Tel & Elec	559.7	23.5	1,366	13
17	15	Dow Chemical	555.7	–9.3	1,034	17
18	19	E I du Pont	545.1	18.7	1,269	15
19	17	Intl Tel & Tel	540.5	15.5	927	20
20	22	Phillips Petroleum	516.9	25.6	854	21

Determining
Funding Priorities
of Local Corporations

Unlike foundations, corporations are not required to disclose information about past grants or funding priorities. The exceptions are corporations who have established foundations to administer their grants.

Foundation Center National Data Book, Volume I

Foundation Center
888 Seventh Avenue
New York, NY 10019

With your list of local corporations, visit The Foundation Center or a regional foundation collection. Check the **National Data Book,** Volume I, for foundations whose names approximate the corporations on your list. For example, Gillette Company's foundation is Gillette Charitable and Educational Foundation.

This method is not foolproof, since some corporate foundation names are quite different from the corporate sponsor. For example, Shawmut Bank of Boston's giving arm is Warren Charitable Trust.

Once you've identified the existence of a corporate foundation, refer to their 990 tax return (see the section on **Researching Foundations** for more information about the 990s).

Handbook of Corporate Social Responsibility: Profiles of Involvement ($42)

prepared by Human Resources Network
Chilton Books
Radnor, PA

The Handbook includes descriptions of sample projects that some of the large corporations have funded. Because of its price, fundraisers should find someone who has already purchased it. The Foundation Center and some of the regional collections have it available for public use.

Business and Society Review ($34/year)

Warren, Gorham and Lamont, Inc.
870 Seventh Avenue
New York, NY 10019

This periodical is devoted to discussions of corporate social responsibility and frequently publishes informa-

tion on social responsibility activities of specific companies. It covers everything from investment practices and affirmative action to loaned-executive programs and grants.

Other
Information
About
Corporations

Annual Reports (free from individual corporations)

Financial information, glowing descriptions of the company's operations and products, names of directors and top officers appear in a corporation's annual report. There are precious few, though, that describe their corporate giving program, or even mention the total grants made during the year.

Official Summary of Security Transactions and Holdings

U.S. Securities and Exchange Commission
Washington, D.C. 20549

The Summary is published monthly by the government watchdog agency, the Securities and Exchange Commission. When an officer, director or individual shareholder owning 5% or more of the corporation's stock buys or sells any shares, the transaction appears in the Summary, along with their total holdings. The Summary is arranged by corporation names; researchers can compute the value of the stock by multiplying the number of shares by the current market price found in either the Summary or in the stock pages of major newspapers.

Fundraisers for colleges and hospitals have used this information in approaching top corporate executives; community organizers use the Summary to research the wealth and power of corporate officials. Fundraisers for small citizen groups might want to use the Summary to research the wealth of individuals who have a known interest in the area the group is working in.

Sample:

OFFICIAL SUMMARY OF SECURITY TRANSACTIONS AND HOLDINGS

72

ISSUER SECURITY REPORTING PERSON NATURE OF OWNERSHIP	Relationship	Date of transaction	Character	Late, amended or inconsistent	TRANSACTIONS				Month end holdings of securities	Option reported
					Bought or otherwise acquired		Sold or otherwise disposed of			
					Amount	Price	Amount	Price		
FIRST NATL BOSTON CORP										
COM										
BROWN WILLIAM L	OD									
DIRECT....................		10/24/77							1,171	
DIRECT....................		10/24/77	P		21	$26.69			1,192	
INDIRECT..................		10/24/77	B		71				833	
INDIRECT..................		10/24/77							833	
HILL RICHARD D	CB									
DIRECT....................		10/24/77							2,099	
INDIRECT..................		10/24/77	P		93	$27.63			2,904	
PHALEN GEORGE F	OD									
DIRECT....................		10/24/77							819	
INDIRECT..................		10/24/77	B		47				510	
PUTNAM DAVID F	D									
DIRECT....................		10/24/77	T		7				426	

Official Summary
of security transactions
and holdings

VOLUME 43, NUMBER 11

for the period
October 12, 1977 to
November 10, 1977

United States Securities and Exchange Commission
Washington, D. C. 20549

Who's Who in America

Marquis Who's Who, Inc.
200 East Ohio Street
Chicago, IL 60611

Several Who's Who volumes are published every year including **Who's Who in America** and **Who's Who in Business and Finance**. Who's Who is useful for getting brief biographical information on top corporate executives. Where they went to school, what clubs they belong to, names of directorships in corporations and nonprofit groups, and home addresses are included.

Sample:

MARTIN, JAMES RUSSELL, life ins. co. exec.; b. Peoria, Ill., Dec. 3, 1918; s. Ray and Gertrude Irene (Tilley) M.; B.S. in Bus. Administrn., U. Ill. 1940; m. Minnie Woodward Faucett, Mar. 6, 1942; children Sally Lee, James Philip. With Home Life Ins. Co. N.Y., 1940-41, 46-51, mgr., Rochester, N.Y., 1950-51; with Mass. Mut. Life Ins. Co., Springfield, 1951 , 2d v.p., 1958-62, v.p. agy. sales, 1962-67, sr. v.p., 1967-68, pres., chief exec. officer, 1968-74, chmn., chief exec., 1974 -, also dir., chmn. exec. com. of bd. dirs.; dir. 1st Nat. Bank Boston, 1st Boston Corp., Mississippi River Corp. Mem. adv. com. Woodrow Wilson Internat. Center for Scholars. Trustee Pioneer Valley United Fund, Springfield United Fund; bd. dirs. Jr. Achievement of Springfield, Inc.; trustee Eastern States Expn.; corporator Springfield Coll.; bd. overseers Crotched Mountain Found. Served to lt. col. USAAF, 1941-46. Mem. Nat. Assn. Life Underwriters, Am. Coll. Life Underwriters, Kappa Sigma. Republican. Home: 231 Knollwood Dr Longmeadow MA 01106 Office: 1295 State St Springfield MA

Forms 10-K and 8-K

U.S. Securities and Exchange Commission
Washington, D.C. 20459

These reports are filed with the Securities and Exchange Commission by corporations that sell stock on the New York and American stock exchanges. These reports are available at SEC offices, large university libraries and most business school libraries. Contribution amounts don't appear on the form, but a description of the corporation's operations, its directors and locations of subsidiary companies are included. Portions of a Form 10-K are reproduced here:

SECURITIES AND EXCHANGE COMMISSION

Washington, D. C. 20549

FORM 10-K

ANNUAL REPORT PURSUANT TO SECTION 13 OR 15(d)
OF THE SECURITIES EXCHANGE ACT OF 1934

For the fiscal year ended December 31, 1977   Commission File No. 1-7254

SAXON INDUSTRIES, INC.

(Exact name of Registrant as specified in its charter)

Delaware	**13-5369500**
(State or other jurisdiction of incorporation or organization)	(I.R.S. Employer Identification Number)
1230 Avenue of the Americas, New York, N. Y.	**10020**
(Address of principal executive office)	(Zip Code)

(212) 246-9500

(Registrant's telephone number including area code)

Item 1. *Parent and Subsidiaries.*

The Registrant, a Delaware corporation, has the following wholly-owned subsidiaries:

	Jurisdiction of Incorporation
The Chukerman Company	Illinois
Copystatics Manufacturing Corporation	New York
Gamma Packaging Corp.	New York
E. Greene and Company, Inc.	New York
J. F. McCarthy Corp.	New York
Quality Park Products, Inc.	New Jersey

Item 11. *Executive Officers of the Registrant.*

The executive officers of the registrant are:

Name	Office and Period of Continuous Service	Age (as of 12/31/77)
Stanley Lurie	President since June 1977, and Director. An executive officer and Director since 1968.	57
Philip K. Koss	Executive Vice President and Director, since 1953.	61
Bruce D. Tobin	Senior Vice President, since January 1978. Previously, Vice President since 1970 and Vice President and General Manager since 1971 of the Company's subsidiary, Standard Packaging Corporation.	43

Where to Find Information about Corporations

Public libraries

Reference departments usually house the major resource books about corporations, such as Standard and Poor's, Dun and Bradstreet's, **Who's Who,** and sometimes Moody's Manuals. Some large public libraries have special business collections such as the Kirstein Library, the business branch of Boston Public Library in Massachusetts.

University libraries

Reference departments have the standard research materials. Some microfilm departments of large university libraries have the Form 10-K reports filed by corporations with the Securities and Exchange Commission.

Business School libraries

Resource materials on corporations are usually quite extensive, including directories, annual reports, the **Official Summary of Security Transactions and Holdings,** and Form 10-K reports.

Frequently Asked Questions About Corporate Giving

Frequently Asked Questions About Corporate Giving

1. *MANY CORPORATIONS DON'T GIVE MONEY TO NONPROFIT GROUPS. ARE THERE OTHER TYPES OF ASSISTANCE THEY CAN PROVIDE?*

   Here are some ways corporations help citizen groups, aside from grants. There are many others, so talk with other organizations for more ideas.

   - **Printing:** Large businesses that use lots of forms, like insurance companies, are apt to have their own printing press in the basement. Ask if they'll print your brochure, booklets, annual reports or other one-time only publications. Occasionally, businesses will help groups do some of the pre-printing work, such as layout and design.

   - **Loaned executive programs:** A few corporations give their employees "leaves-of-absence" to work full-time with nonprofit organizations. More common are programs that enable employees to donate a few hours per week with community groups. For example, an accountant can help a nonprofit set up its bookkeeping system or someone from a company's advertising department could help prepare brochures and media campaign strategies. If you ask for this kind of assistance, make sure the employee is familiar with your needs and how nonprofits operate in general, especially in the accounting area.

   - **Product contributions:** The 1976 Tax Reform Act allows corporations to deduct only the manufacturing cost of products, so this type of donation is less attractive to corporations than it used to be. But many still do donate their products (e.g. Polaroid gives away its cameras) to nonprofits if they are to be used for "exempt purposes" and not re-sold.

   - **Use of corporate facilities:** Providing space for conferences and meetings, and telephones for fundraising telethons are common corporate contributions.

   - **Free legal help:** Some law firms allow their employees to do a certain percentage of *pro bono publico* (free) work. This is particularly helpful for new citizen groups who are muddling through the incorporation process and applying for tax-exempt status.

   - **Used office furniture:** Corporations that are moving to new office space or remodeling their present space often donate desks chairs, tables, or filing cabinets. Urban citizen groups should keep an eye on new skyscrapers under construction, find out who's moving in, and call the businesses for used furniture.

   - **Billboard space:** Advertising companies that lease billboard space may be willing to donate a billboard or two for short-term use by community groups.

   - **Newspaper ads:** Some newspapers donate advertising space for special events, usually for one or two days.

- **Transportation:** Delivery services and other large transportation users sometimes donate their used vans to nonprofit organizations. More frequent, however, is the loan of vans (sometimes with drivers) for a one-time event.

- **Paper:** With the increasing use of computers, businesses usually have tons of used computer printout paper. Many recycle the paper and some give it to groups, such as day care centers, for children to use. Donations from paper and printing companies include paper of all sizes, types and colors. It may be odd-size paper, colored posterboard from a printing over-run or plain writing paper.

2. *AFTER DOING ALL THE RESEARCH ON LOCAL CORPORATIONS, IT SEEMS IMPOSSIBLE TO TELL WHAT THEY WILL FUND AND WHO TO CONTACT FOR INFORMATION. HOW SHOULD FUNDRAISERS APPROACH CORPORATIONS?*

Some companies have established foundations to administer their contributions, in which case they are required to file a Form 990 Tax Return with the Internal Revenue Service (see the section on **Researching Foundations** for more information). The 990s contain a list of grant recipients, names of contact people, and other financial information.

The Handbook of Corporate Social Responsibility: Profiles of Involvement (prepared by Human Resources Network), has descriptions of some corporate giving programs. For other corporations, you probably won't find much information about who is eligible for funding, an unfortunate fact of life. You can assume, though, that if a corporation does make grants, about half will go to United Way and a good portion of the remainder to colleges and hospitals. If you can show how your project will benefit the corporation's employees and the community, you may have a better chance.

Finding a person to talk with in a corporation is sometimes even more frustrating. The activity in this section focuses on how to involve members of citizen groups in approaching employees of corporations,

a method commonly used by well-established nonprofit organizations. If a group member does know an employee, that person often has an easier time finding out how to contact the right persons and how corporate gifts are handled. Another approach is to call a corporation's public relations or public affairs department and ask for the person in charge of corporate gifts. This is the easiest and least time-consuming method of getting information.

3. *SOME CORPORATIONS RESPOND TO INFORMATION PHONE CALLS BY SAYING THAT 'ALL OUR FUNDS ARE COMMITTED FOR THE YEAR.' IS THIS TRUE AND WHAT DOES IT MEAN?*

Unfortunately, it is usually true. Corporations establish annual corporate gift budgets and often designate recipients early in their fiscal year. So citizen groups should find out what fiscal year the corporation is operating on by writing for a copy of their annual report. Phone calls can then be made and proposals sent a few months prior to the beginning of the corporation's fiscal year.

4. *WHAT IS THE APPLICATION PROCESS FOR CORPORATE GIVING?*

Like foundations, most corporations do not have application forms. This means that citizen groups can design their own proposal, and the format suggested in **Program Planning and Proposal Writing**, by Norton Kiritiz, (Grantsmanship Center) is a good one for corporations. For local corporations, the proposals should be short, usually no more than 10-15 pages.

The most common method of approaching corporations is to begin with telephone calls to find the person in charge of corporate giving. This call is for informational purposes and not usually an actual request for money. The proposal is then submitted, with a cover letter that ends by saying that the applicant will be calling in a few weeks to find out the status of the proposal. Then, as promised, the follow-up phone call is made. Some corporations are willing to interview applicants, which usually occurs after the written proposal has been reviewed by the corporation.

Fundraisers for citizen groups have traditionally had to "go it alone." They get the support but rarely the active participation of their policy-making boards and members. One way to involve more people in the fundraising process is to ask board members to contact people they know who work for prospective corporate donors, either by asking for information about the corporate gifts program or making an appeal for funds. The extent of involvement depends on the willingness and skills of the member.

This method is commonly used by fundraisers for large institutions, but citizen groups usually assume that they have no contacts with prospective corporations. This activity focuses on how to determine whether or not citizen group members have "contacts" within corporations. The activity can be done during a board meeting or mailed to each individual member of the organization to fill out on their own.

_____

Suggested Follow-Up: The fundraiser should work closely with the members, making sure that tasks are accomplished and making suggestions about what to say. When the members have completed their tasks, you could arrange for a "war story" lunch — a time for people who've helped out with the corporate appeals to share their experiences. This is often an amusing and instructive way to acquaint other members with corporate fundraising.

Reprinted from Workforce

Exercise:
The Corporate Connection

The Process:

1. Compile a list of corporate prospects with the names of top executives as on the sample contact survey.
2. Introduce the contact survey to the organization's members with some explanatory comments about how it will be used.
3. Ask each person to fill out the survey, adding comments they think will be helpful like, "I went to school with him," or "She's my next door neighbor."
4. When the completed surveys have been returned, sit down with each member and discuss strategy.
    *   Will the member call his/her contact for information about corporate giving policies?
    *   Will (s)he call the contact and arrange for an appointment?
    *   Will (s)he write a letter saying that a proposal is on the way and arrange for an interview?
    *   Will (s)he call or write a letter of introduction for the fundraiser?
5. Make sure that the member is clear on what (s)he is supposed to do and a deadline is set for completing the task.

140

Sample Contact Survey

Put a check beside the names of people you know or are acquainted with, and write the names of other employees you know. Please return these contact survey sheets to me by _____.
The * denotes membership on the corporation's board of directors.

CH = Chairman of the Board	Pres = President
CEO = Chief Executive Officer	VP = Vice President

KNOW WELL	ACQUAINTED WITH	HAVE A FRIEND WHO KNOWS	
			First National Bank of Boston
____	____	____	*Richard D. Hill, CH
____	____	____	*William L. Brown, Pres
____	____	____	*Gerhard D. Bleicken, CH John Hancock
____	____	____	*Joseph R. Carter, Pres Wyman-Gordon
____	____	____	*Robert A. Charpie, Pres Cabot Corp.
____	____	____	*Alice Emerson, Pres Wheaton College
____	____	____	*James R. Martin, CH Mass. Mutual
____	____	____	*William C. Mercer, Pres N.E. Telephone
____	____	____	*Colman M. Mockler, CH, CEO Gillette
____	____	____	*J Donald Monan, Pres Boston College
____	____	____	*George E. Phalen, Exec VP
____	____	____	*Richard A. Smith, Pres General Cinema
____	____	____	*Ben Ames Williams, Exec VP
____	____	____	T. McLean Griffin, Sr VP, Counsel
____	____	____	Kenneth R. Rossano, Sr VP, Development
			Names of other employees:

(This is a partial list for sample use only.)

Conclusion

These last chapters have dealt with some aspects of raising money from corporations, foundations, the public sector, churches and the community. Since it's easy to get bogged down in the "nuts-and-bolts" of raising money, some "goals for fundraisers" are listed below as a gentle reminder that fund-raising is a means to an end.

Goals for Fundraisers

- **Concentrate on future-oriented fund-raising.**

  Much of the fund-raising by citizen groups is crisis-oriented. A good dose of planning, prioritizing programs, and a cautious allocation of resources are some of the measures groups can take. Consult materials listed in the **Resource Section** under **Program Planning** for more information.

- **Regard money as only one of many resources.**

  "Resource mobilization" is a concept that involves cataloguing resources that an organization already has access to and resources that are needed to run programs. Many supplies can be donated, volunteers recruited, resources exchanged between nonprofit organizations and student interns recruited from local universities and vocational education schools. These are some of the ways that needs can be met without requiring money.

Reprinted from the Children's Yellow Pages, Holyoke, Mass.

142

- **Work toward the solution of problems rather than building an organization.**

  Much of the current fund-raising is directed toward expanding organizations and creating permanent institutions. Programs need to be designed that will decrease people's dependency on services.

- **Work toward community problem-solving and self-reliance.**

  — *What is your group's relationship to the issues and problems of the community as a whole?*

  — *How will your group develop cooperation with other organizations in the community?*

  — *How do the activities of your group increase the decision-making power of community residents?*

These questions focus on building a community power base rather than an institutional power base. Contact the Institute for Local Self-Reliance (1717 18th Street, N.W., Washington, D.C. 20009) for information about community self-sufficiency projects across the country.

- **Add your own goals.**

We hope that you will share what you learned from this book with others and that your work will be directed toward some of these goals.

Reprinted by permission from the Business and Society Review, Winter 1973-4, No. 8 Copyright 1974 Warren, Gorham and Lamont, Inc. 210 South Street, Boston, Mass. All rights reserved.

Resources

This section includes a variety of resource books and organizations dealing with fund-raising and finances for citizen groups. Consult appropriate chapters for materials used specificially to research possible funding sources.

Accounting and Bookkeeping: Books

Bookkeeping Handbook for Low-Income Groups (free)
National Council of Welfare
Brooke Claxton Building
Ottawa Ontario OK9
Canada

Bookkeeping basics, financial statements, reconciling bank statements and more. A good manual for new or small organizations and for anyone who is struggling with setting up a bookkeeping system.

Financial and Accounting Guide for Nonprofit Organizations ($15)
by Malvern Gross
Ronald Press Company
79 Madison Avenue
New York, NY 10016

Gross is a certified public accountant (CPA) with Price Waterhouse and is the expert on nonprofit accounting. His Guide is excellent and readable, concentrating on different types of accounting systems and options for financial statements. More useful for preparing financial statements than the "nuts-and-bolts" of setting up a bookkeeping system.

Where Do All the $ go? What Every Board and Staff Member of a Nonprofit Organization Should Know About Budgeting ($2.50)
by Gerald G. Bowe, Jr.
New Hampshire Charitable Fund

Drawing by Bonnie Acker, by permission of Hands-On: Guidebook for Appropriate Technology for Massachusetts, 1978.

One South Street
Concord, NH 03301

A good training manual for everyone with clear explanations of accounting terms and budgeting methods.

Church Funding: Books

"A Study of Religious Recipts and Expenditures in the U.S."

Interfaith Research Committee of the Commission

on Private Philanthropy
and Public Needs
Research Papers, Volume
I, History, Trends and
Current Magnitudes, pp.
365 - 450
Superintendent of Documents
Government Printing
Office
Washington, D.C. 20402

One of the few studies of church-giving, with lots of data on each major denomination.

"Philanthropy and the Powerless"
Sarah C. Carey
Research Papers, Volume II, Philanthropic Fields of Interest, Additional Perspectives, pp. 1141-1144
Superintendent of Documents
Government Printing
Office
Washington, D.C. 20402

A brief look at specific examples of church-giving to the poor and the powerless.

Corporations: Books

How to Research Your Local Bank ($2.00)
by William Batko
Institute for Local Self-Reliance
1717 18th Street, N.W.
Washington, D.C. 20009

A well-done "how-to" book, written primarily for community organizers but still relevant for fundraisers.

Open the Books: How to Research a Corporation
Prepared by Urban Planning Aid, Boston, MA
Distributed by Midwest Academy
600 West Fullerton
Chicago, IL 60614

A thorough "how-to" book about researching corporations. Chapters on researching (1) multinational corporations, (2) who controls large corporations, (3) local subsidiaries, (4) real estate companies, and (5) small companies. Each chapter contains background information, sample case studies and materials to use to research corporations. This one was also written primarily for organizers but the research process is the same for fund-raising.

Open The Books

Philanthropy and the Business Corporation ($3.95)
by Marion R. Fremont-Smith
Russell Sage Foundation
230 Park Avenue
New York, NY 10017

Good background on the history and present state of the art of corporate giving.

Stock Ownership and the Control of Corporations ($.60)
by Don Villarejo
New England Free Press
60 Union Square
Somerville, MA 02143

A good study of the largest 250 U.S. industrial corporations and who controls them. Although dated, this is useful for organizers or fundraisers who are researching large corporations.

Corporations: Organizations

The Conference Board
845 Third Avenue
New York, NY 10022

An establishment organization that publishes the **Annual Survey of Corporate Contributions, Corporate Philanthropic Public Service Activities, Social Responsibility and the Smaller Company.**

Council on Economic Priorities
84 Fifth Avenue
New York, NY 10011

The Council researches social responsibility of numerous corporations and publishes a newsletter and other materials.

Intercollegiate Case Clearing House in Boston
Soldiers Field Post Office
Boston, MA 02136

Located at the Harvard Business School, the Clearing House has research case studies on individual corporations. The public may order them at $.50 per copy.

Interfaith Center on Corporate Responsibility
475 Riverside Drive
New York, NY 10027

This organization leads corporate proxy battles and publishes the **Corporate Examiner,** a monthly newsletter ($25) and materials on corporate social responsibility.

Involvement Corps
1785 Massachusetts Avenue, N.W.
Washington, D.C. 20036

IC will help place corporate volunteers in nonprofit organizations across the country.

Foundations: Books

About Foundations How To Find the Facts You Need to Get a Grant ($3.00)
by Judith Margolin
The Foundation Center
888 Seventh Avenue
New York, NY 10019

This is a step-by-step guide to researching foundations, concentrating on Foundation Center materials and 990 Tax Return Forms.

The Bread Game: The Realities of Foundation Funding ($2.95)
by Pacific Change and Regional Young Adult Project
Glide Publications
330 Ellis Street
San Francisco, CA 94102

A short, fun book about the "nature and feeding habits of the beast known as foundations."

Researching Foundations, Part I ($1.55)
Grantsmanship Center
News reprint
1015 West Olympic Boulevard
Los Angeles, CA 90015

Researching Foundations is an in-depth look at some of The Foundation Center's publications, with a section on how to use and not misuse the **Foundation Directory.**

Researching Foundations, Part II ($1.55)
Grantsmanship Center
News reprint
Address same as above

The story of how ace detective, Philicia Malo, helps out her friend, Neda Funz. It's a personal account of her adventures in a foundation library, complete with a description of which books she used and which were most helpful in her search for foundation funding.

Stalking the 990-AR
Grantsmanship Center
News
Issue 12, July-August
1975
Address same as above

This issue is now out of print.
Try the nearest foundation collection for back issues of the News.
This article is an excellent aid in
deciphering the 990 Tax Return
Forms. Although the actual form
has changed since the article was
written, the pieces of information
discussed are everpresent and still
relevant.

Fund-Raising (General): Books

Grants: How to Find Out
About Them and What to
Do Next ($19.50)
by Virginia White
Plenum Press
227 West 17th Street
New York, NY 10011

A good overview of identifying
potential funding sources and
developing a fund-raising
strategy.

The Grantsmanship
Center News ($15/year)
1015 West Olympic
Boulevard
Los Angeles, CA 90015

The News surpasses any other
periodical dealing with grantsmanship. Articles on how federal
agencies review applications,
restrictions on lobbying for nonprofits, program planning and lots
more. Reading the News is a must
for every citizen group.

The Rich and the Super-
Rich ($2.25)
by Ferdinand Lundberg
Bantam Books

A well-documented analysis of who
who owns America with profiles
of selected wealthy families.

The Seven Laws of
Money ($3.95)
by Michael Phillips
Word Wheel and Random
House
New York, NY

This book is a philosophical ex-
ploration of money — how people
relate to it and how people could
relate to it if money didn't make
everyone nervous. If you've read
other books on fund-raising, try
this for a different view. The
author is a former bank vice
president and president of POINT,
the giving arm of the Whole Earth
Catalog.

Fund-Raising (General): Organizations

National Committee for
Responsive Philanthropy
1028 Connecticut Avenue,
N.W., #822
Washington, D.C. 20036

NCRP is a membership organization formed to "focus more
attention on what private philanthropy does and does not do
with its critical dollar resources;
to challenge the secret or in-
accessible decision-making that
determines priorities for many
foundations, corporate giving
programs and federated fund-
raising campaigns; and to work
with individuals and groups who
believe it important to change
grant-giving priorities and procedures..."

Government Funding: Books

The Federal Granting

System: A Guide for
Local Governments in
Massachusetts (free)
Bulletin Center, Cottage A
Thatcher Way
University of Massachu-
setts
Amherst, MA 01003

Prepared by the Mass. Cooperative Extension Service, this
publication contains a good
explanation of the process of
applying for federal funding
and information sources in
Massachusetts.

Federal Programs Mon-
itor ($10/year)
Center for Community
Change
1000 Wisconsin Avenue,N.W.
Washington, D.C. 20007

Community-based programs can
find various articles on legislative activities and funding opportunities for community development projects in this monthly
newsletter.

The Grantsmanship Center
News ($15/year)
1015 West Olympic Boule-
vard
Los Angeles, CA 90015

Along with excellent articles on
all aspects of grantsmanship, the
News (published bimonthly) contains two regular sections on federal funding. "Federal Regulations
Summary" (or, the "authoritative
English translation of the Federal
Register") has information on new
or proposed regulations published
in the Register. "Deadlines" includes upcoming deadlines for selected federal assistance programs.

Newsbriefs ($50/year)
Lutheran Resources
Commission
1346 Connecticut Avenue,
N.W.
Washington, D.C. 20036

With a hefty price tag, Newsbriefs
focuses on legislation for many
types of social service programs,
and includes films and publications on a wide variety of topics.
Citizen groups are better off finding someone who already sub-
scribes to Newsbriefs. The Founda-

tion Center in New York and some
of its regional foundation collections subscribe to the newsletter,
including the Associated Foundation of Greater Boston.

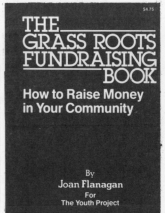

Grassroots Fund-Raising: Books

Direct Mail and Mail
Order Handbook ($43)
by Richard S. Hodgson
The Dartnell Corporation
4660 North Ravenswood
Chicago, IL 60640

A complete explanation of all
aspects of direct mail. Larger
citizen groups for whom direct
mail is a major source of income
will find this a useful reference
source.

Fundraising in the
Public Interest ($5)
by David L. Grubb and
David R. Zwick
Public Citizen, Inc.
P.O. Box 19404
Washington, D.C. 20036

There are three sections in this
book—direct mail canvassing
and marathons for money.
Each is a good introduction to
the topic, although the canvassing section is weak on actual
canvassing techniques.

The Grass Roots Fund-
raising Book: How to
Raise Money in Your
Community ($5.25)
by Joan Flanagan for
The Youth Project

The Swallow Press, Inc.
P.O. Box 988
Hicksville, NY 18802

An exciting and inspiring book on all aspects of community fund-raising. The major emphasis is on planning fund-raising events that are fun and profitable. It's both fun to read and very complete.

Handbook of Special Events for Nonprofit Organizations, Tested Ideas for Fund Raising and Public Relations ($13.45)
by Edwin R. Leibert and Bernice E. Sheldon
Taft Products
1000 Vermont Avenue,N.W.
Washington, D.C. 20005

A good overview of planning large fund-raising events.

Spend Less, Raise More. A Cost-Conscious Look at Direct Mail ($1)
by Elizabeth Broder Peterson
Direct Mail Fundraisers Association
810 Seventh Avenue
New York, NY 10019

Covers the basics of direct mail with hints on techniques that work well and those that don't.

Incorporation: Books

Funding for Social Change, Volume I: How to Become An Employer and Gain Tax Exempt Status ($3.20)
by Stella Alvo and Kate Shackford
Funding for Social Change
175 West 92nd Street
New York, NY 10025

Prepared in 1977, this guide includes information on incorporation, applying for tax exemption, and the responsibilities of being an employer.

Nonprofit Arts Organization: Formation and Maintenance ($13)
Bay Area Lawyers for the Arts
25 Taylor Street
San Francisco, CA 94102

Model bylaws and articles of incorporation are included in this volume about becoming a nonprofit organization. Other aspects of maintaining tax exempt status are mentioned as well.

Program Planning: Books

Establishment of a Long-Range Planning Capability ($4.00)
by S.H. Dole, G.H. Fisher, E.D. Harris, and J. String, Fr.
The Rand Corporation

This RAND study contains useful information on long-range planning techniques.

Evaluation Research: Methods of Assessing Program Effectiveness ($4.95)
by Carol H. Weiss
Prentice-Hall

Evaluation Research is a good

overview of the purposes and types of evaluations. The book focuses on how to define what is being measured, designing the evaluation, and deciding how the data will be used.

Goal Analysis ($2.95)
By Robert Mager
Fearon Publishers
6 Davis Drive
Belmont, CA 94002

A good guide for writing goals statements that will be useful rather than those that collect dust on a shelf. Techniques for clarifying "fuzzy" goals and making them achievable are included.

1001 Catalog—Techniques and Strategies for Successful Action Programs ($6.50)
American Association of University Women
2401 Virginia Avenue, N.W.
Washington, D.C. 20037

A catalog of approaches and techniques useful on planning and executing projects.

Planning, for a Change
by Duane Dale and Nancy Mitiguy
Citizen Involvement Training Project
138 Hasbrouck, Continuing Education
University of Massachusetts
Amherst, MA 01003

Activities focusing on all phases of developing programs; program planning models, how to get all the program options on the table, selecting an appropriate program, and how to get a program off the ground.

Proposal Writing: Books

Developing Skills in Proposal Writing ($10)
by Mary Hall
Continuing Education Publications
1633 S.W. Park
Portland, Oregon 97207

Although this was written in 1971, this is still one of the best books about the proposal-writing process.

Grants: How to Find Out About Them and What to do Next ($19.50)
by Virginia White
Plenum Press
227 West 17th Street
New York, NY 10011

This is an excellent introduction to fund-raising and a good explanation of the application process, including comments on pre and post-application steps.

How to Prepare a Research Proposal ($2.95 plus postage)
Syracuse University Bookstore
303 University Place
Syracuse, NY 13210

Good for citizen groups who are preparing research proposals.

Preparing Instructional Objectives, 2nd edition ($3.95)
by Robert Mager
Fearon Publishers
6 Davis Drive
Belmont, CA 94002

If writing specific, measurable objectives is a problem for you, Mager's book is a short fun way to improve your skills. Although written for educators, the material is easily adaptable for any kind of nonprofit organization.